Collins
HANDY ROAD ATLAS
SCOTLAND

Handwritten: 99p / 15

D1099949

KEY TO MAP PAGES

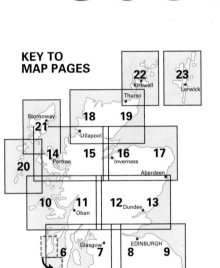

CONTENTS

Road Maps at 9 miles to 1 inch	2-23
Urban Area Maps at 4 miles to 1 inch	24-25
Aberdeen, Dundee,	24
Edinburgh, Glasgow	25
Index to place names	**26-30**
Street maps of city centres	**31-72**
Key to street map pages	31
Aberdeen	32-35
Index to Aberdeen	36-37
Dundee	38-39
Index to Dundee	40-41
Edinburgh	42-51
Index to Edinburgh	52-57
Glasgow	58-65
Index to Glasgow	66-72
Radio Stations	Inside back cover

Published by Collins
An imprint of HarperCollinsPublishers
77-85 Fulham Palace Road, Hammersmith, London W6 8JB

www.collins.co.uk

Copyright © HarperCollinsPublishers Ltd 2004

Collins® is a registered trademark of HarperCollinsPublishers Limited

Mapping generated from Collins Bartholomew digital databases   e-mail: roadcheck@harpercollins.co.uk

Mapping on pages 32-35, 42-51 and 58-65 uses map data licenced from Ordnance Survey® with the permission of the Controller of Her Majesty's Stationery Office. © Crown copyright. Licence number 399302

The grid on the mapping pages 24-25, 32-35, 38-39, 42-51 and 58-65 is the National Grid taken from the Ordnance Survey map with the permission of the controller of Her Majesty's Stationery Office.

Printed in Hong Kong   ISBN 0 00 716954X   Imp 002   QC11596   BDM

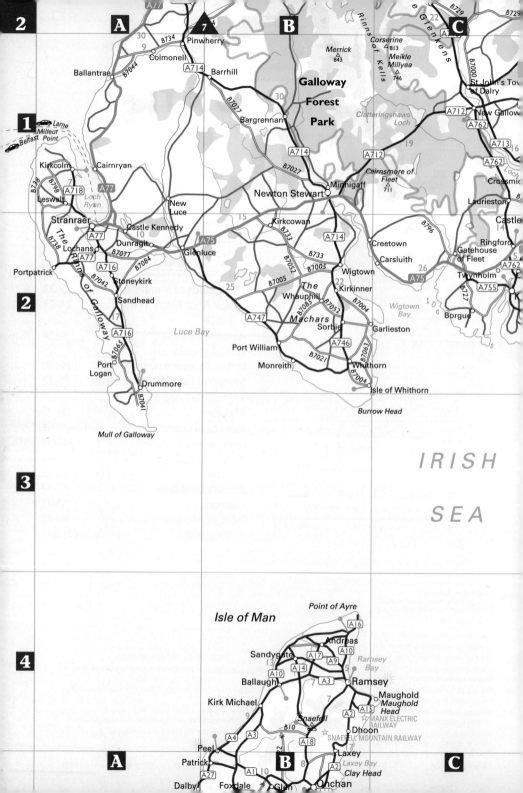

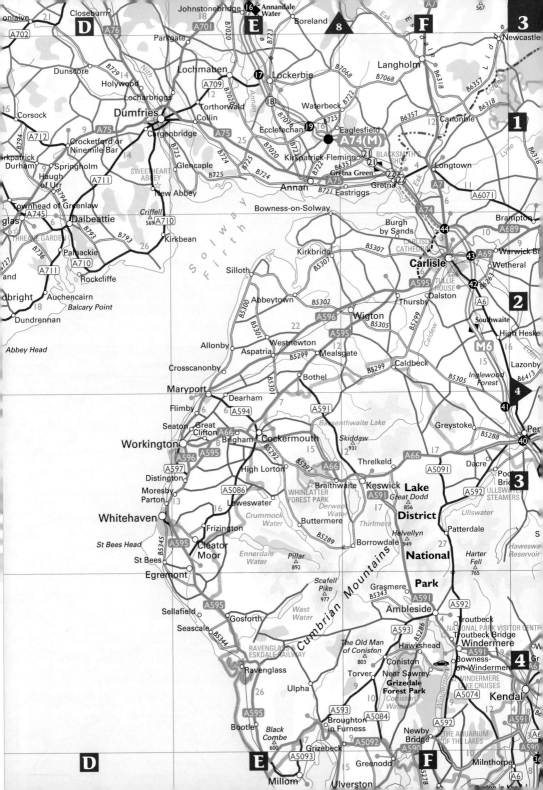

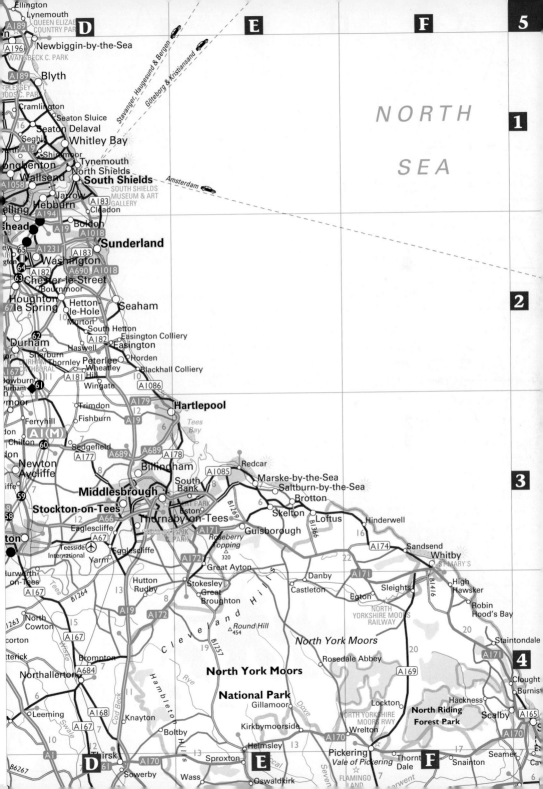

D **E** **F** **5**

Ellington
Lynemouth
QUEEN ELIZABETH
COUNTRY PARK
A189
A196 Newbiggin-by-the-Sea
WANSBECK C. PARK

NORTH

1

A189 Blyth

PLESSEY
WOODS C. PARK

Cramlington
Seaton Sluice
Seaton Delaval
Seghill
Shiremoor Whitley Bay

SEA

Longbenton Tynemouth
Wallsend North Shields
Jarrow **South Shields**
A1058
SOUTH SHIELDS
MUSEUM & ART
GALLERY
Hebburn A183 Cleadon
A194 Boldon
Gateshead A9
A1018

65 A1231 **Sunderland**
A183
64 Washington
63 A182 A690 A1018
Chester-le-Street
Bournmoor

2

Houghton
le Spring Hetton
le-Hole Seaham
Murton
South Hetton
62 Easington Colliery
Durham Haswell Easington
Sherburn
Thornley Peterlee Horden
Thornley Wheatley
61 Hill Blackhall Colliery
Wingate A1086

Trimdon A179 **Hartlepool**
Fishburn 12
A19 Tees
6 Bay 7

A(M) Sedgefield
Chilton 60 A177 A689 A178
Newton 8
Aycliffe Billingham Redcar

3

59 **Middlesbrough** South Marske-by-the-Sea
Stockton-on-Tees Bank Saltburn-by-the-Sea
58 12 A66 A1085 Brotton
Egglescliffe Thornaby-on-Tees Skelton
Teesside A67 A171 Guisborough Loftus Hinderwell
International Egglescliffe Roseberry 16 A174 Sandsend
Yarm A172 Topping Whitby
320 ST MARY'S
A167 Great Ayton Danby A171 High
on-Tees Hutton Castleton Sleights Hawsker
A167 Rudby Stokesley Egton B1416 Robin
B1264 Great NORTH Hood's Bay
Broughton YORKSHIRE MOORS
A9 A172 RAILWAY 20 Staintondale
North Round Hill A171
Cowton 454 **North York Moors** 20

4

A167 19 A169
Brompton Rosedale Abbey Hackness
A684 **North York Moors** North Riding Burnis
Northallerton Forest Park Scalby
A168 **National Park** A165
Leeming Gillamoor Lockton A70
A167 Kirkbymoorside Wrelton
Knayton NORTH YORKSHIRE
Boltby MOORS RWY
Helmsley 13 A70 Thornt 17 Seamer
Thirsk Sproxton Pickering Dale Snainton
D Vale of Pickering **E** **F**
Sowerby FLAMINGO
Wass LAND
Oswaldkirk
B6267

Stavanger, Haugesund & Bergen
Göteborg & Kristiansand
Amsterdam

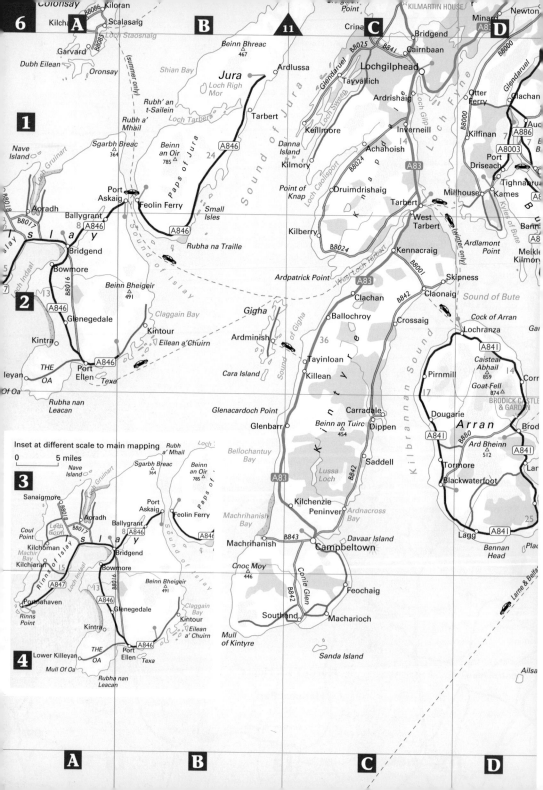

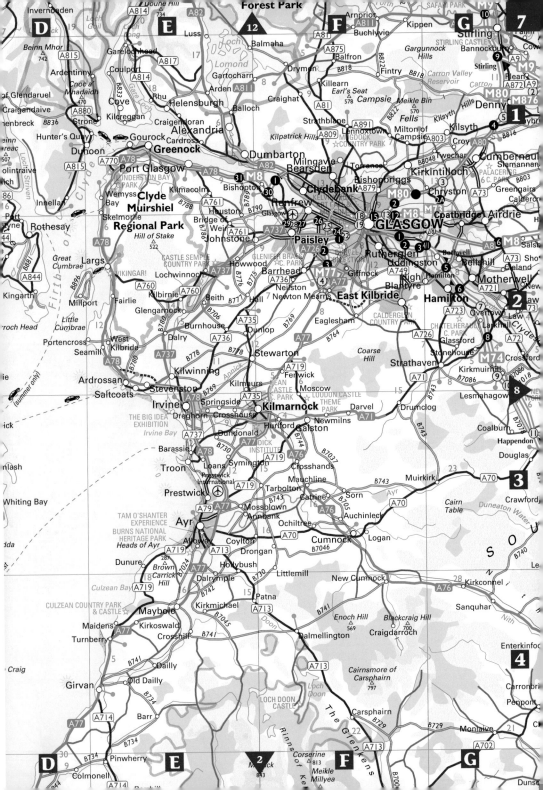

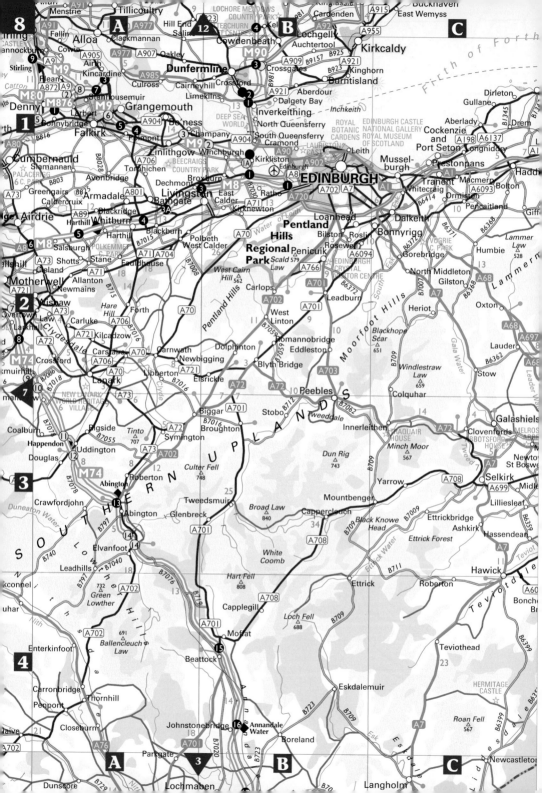

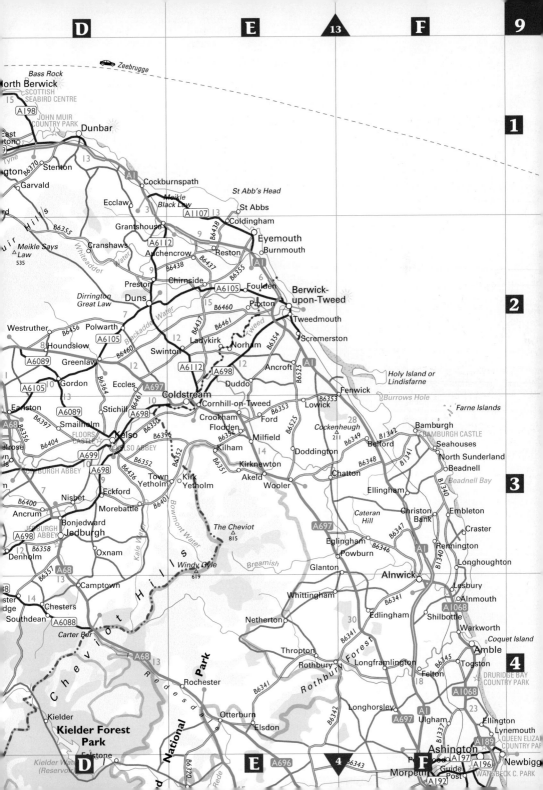

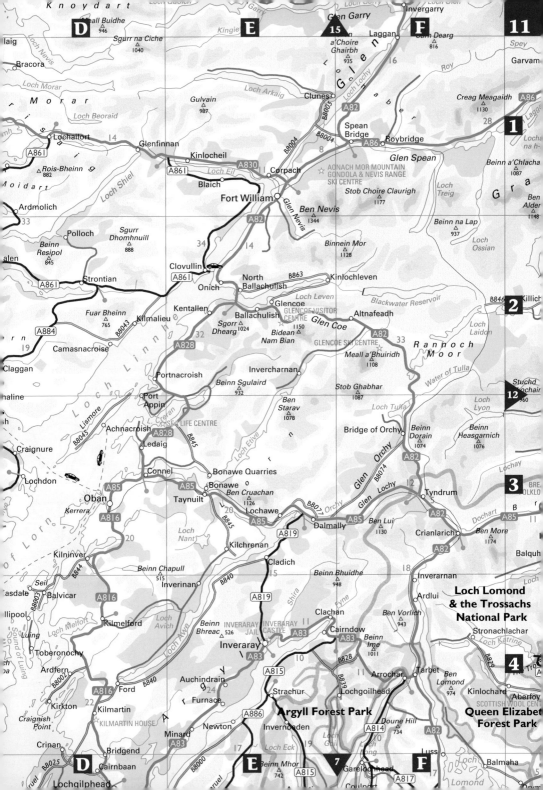

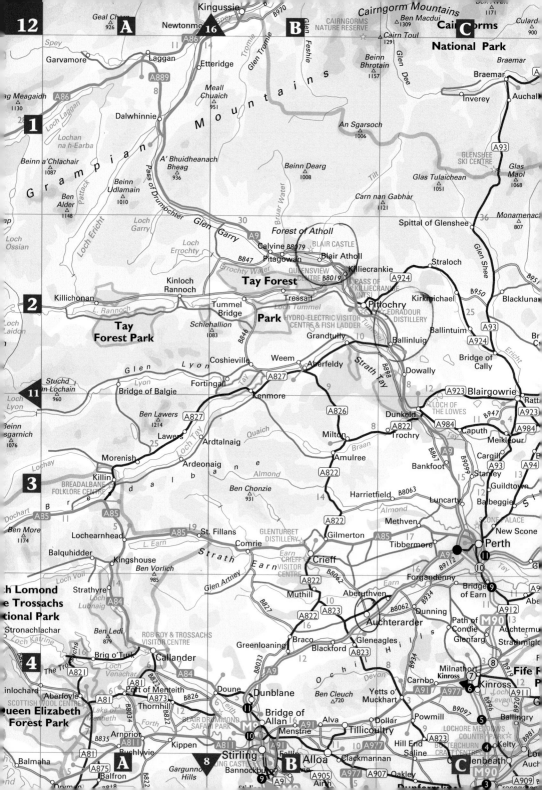

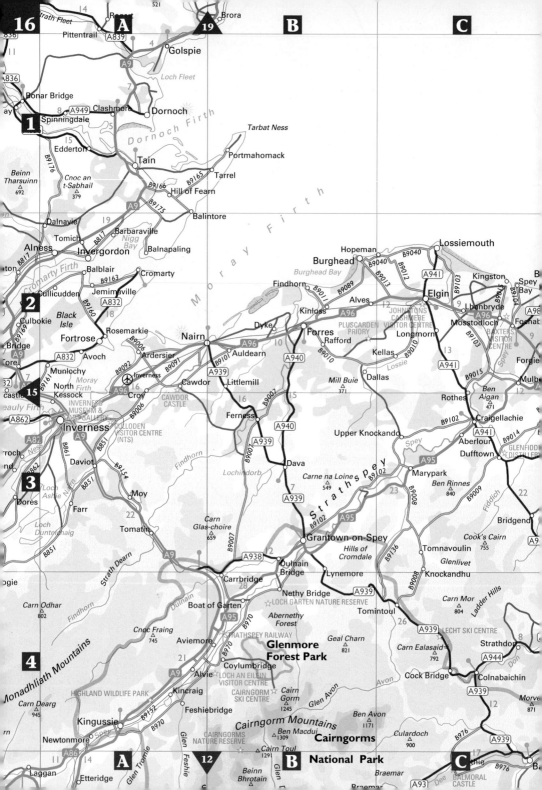

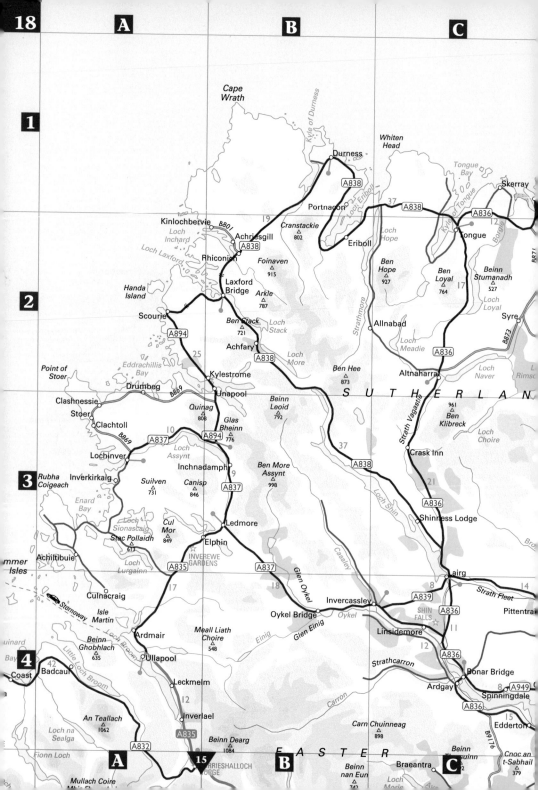

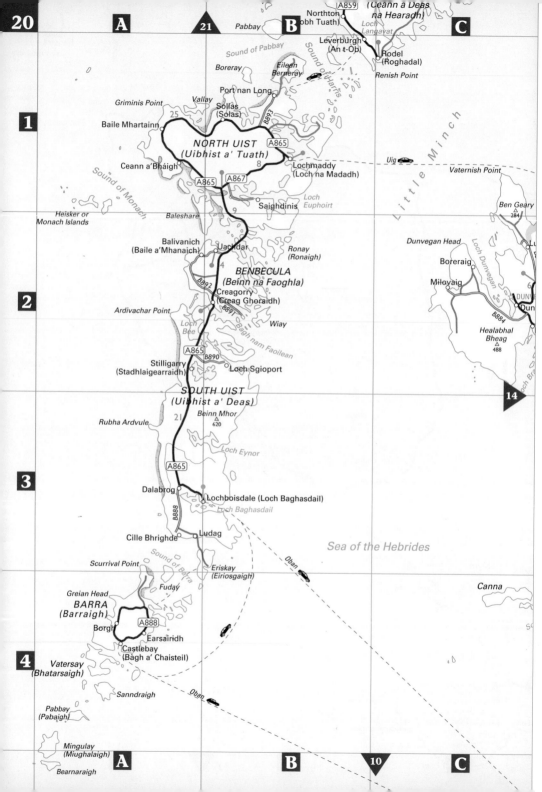

Pabbay

(Ceann a Deas na Hearadh)

A859

Northton
obh Tuath)

Loch
Langavat

Sound of Pabbay

Leverburgh
(An t-Ob)

Boreray

Eilean
Berneray

Rodel
(Roghadal)

Sound of Harris

Renish Point

Griminis Point

Vallay

Port nan Long

Sollas
(Solas)

25

Baile Mhartainn

**NORTH UIST
(Uibhist a' Tuath)**

8

Little Minch

B893

A865

Ceann a'Bhaigh

A865

A867

Lochmaddy
(Loch na Madadh)

Uig

Vaternish Point

Heisker or
Monach Islands

Baleshare

Saighdinis

Loch
Euphoirt

Ben Geary
284

Dunvegan Head

Balivanich
(Baile a'Mhanaich)

Uachdar

Ronay
(Ronaigh)

Boreraig

Lu

Milovaig

DUNV
Dun

**BENBECULA
(Beinn na Faoghla)**

B892

Creagorry
(Creag Ghoraidh)

B891

Wiay

B884

Ardivachar Point

Loch
Bee

Bàgh nam Faoilean

Healabhal
Bheag
488

A865

B890

Stilligarry
(Stadhlaigearraidh)

Loch Sgioport

14

**SOUTH UIST
(Uibhist a' Deas)**

Rubha Ardvule

21

Beinn Mhor
620

Loch Eynor

A865

Dalabrog

Lochboisdale (Loch Baghasdail)

Loch Baghasdail

B888

Cille Bhrighde

Ludag

Sea of the Hebrides

Scurrival Point

Sound of Barra

Eriskay
(Eiriosgaigh)

Oban

Canna

Greian Head

Fuday

**BARRA
(Barraigh)**

Borgh

A888

Earsairidh

Castlebay
(Bàgh a' Chaisteil)

Vatersay
(Bhatarsaigh)

Sanndraigh

Oban

Pabbay
(Pabaigh)

Mingulay
(Miughalaigh)

Bearnaraigh

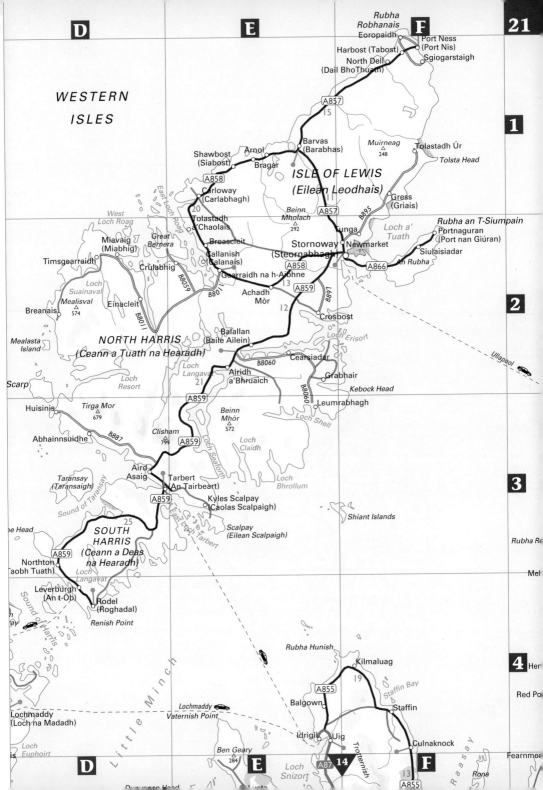

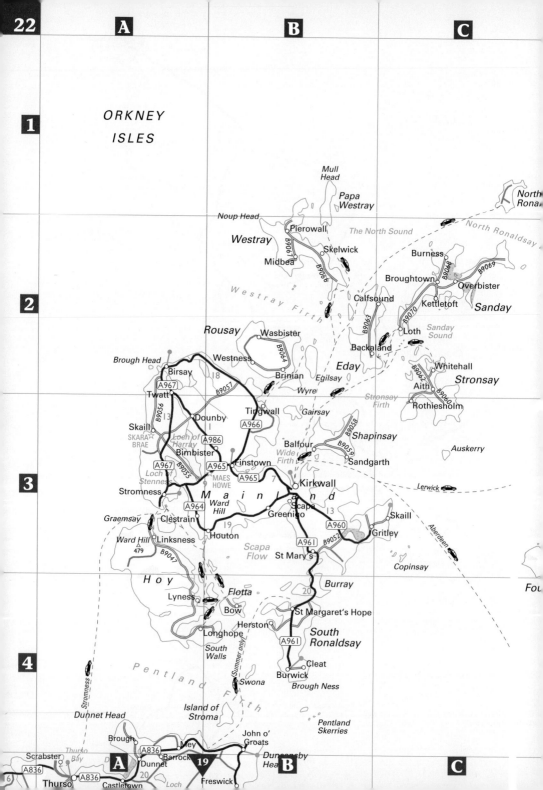

A　　**B**　　**C**

1

*ORKNEY
ISLES*

Mull
Head

*Papa
Westray*

North
Rona...

Noup Head

Pierowall

Westray　　The North Sound

North Ronaldsay

Skelwick

Midbea

B9067

B9066

Burness

Broughtown

B9058

B9069

Overbister

Calfsound

Kettletoft

Sanday

2

W e s t r a y   F i r t h

B9063

B9070

Loth

*Sanday
Sound*

Rousay

Wasbister

Backaland

Eday

Whitehall

Stronsay

Westness

B9064

Brinian

Egilsay

Aith

B9062

B9060

Rothiesholm

Brough Head

Birsay

18

Wyre

Gairsay

*Stronsay
Firth*

A967

B9057

Tingwall

Twatt

B9056

13

Dounby

A966

B9058

Shapinsay

Skaill

SKARA☆
BRAE

*Loch of
Harray*

A986

Balfour

Sandgarth

B9059

Auskerry

Bimbister

A967

A965

Finstown

*Wide
Firth*

Loch of
Stenness

B9055

MAES
HOWE

A965

7

Kirkwall

Lerwick

3

Stromness

A964

*Ward
Hill*

Scapa

Greenigo

13

Skaill

M a i n l a n d

Graemsay

Clestrain

19

Houton

A960

Gritley

Aberdeen

Ward Hill
△
479

Linksness

B9047

*Scapa
Flow*

A961

B9052

St Mary's

Copinsay

Fou...

H o y

Lyness

Flotta

Bow

Burray

20

Burray

St Margaret's Hope

Longhope

Herston

A961

*South
Ronaldsay*

4

*South
Walls*

Summer only

Cleat

Burwick

P e n t l a n d

Swona

Brough Ness

Dunnet Head

Stromness

*Island of
Stroma*

John o'
Groats

*Pentland
Skerries*

F i r t h

Brough

Mey

A836

Barrock

Duncansby
Hea...

Scrabster

*Thurso
Bay*

D...

Dunnet

A　　**19**　　**B**

C

A836

6

Thurso

A836

Castletown

20

Loch

Freswick

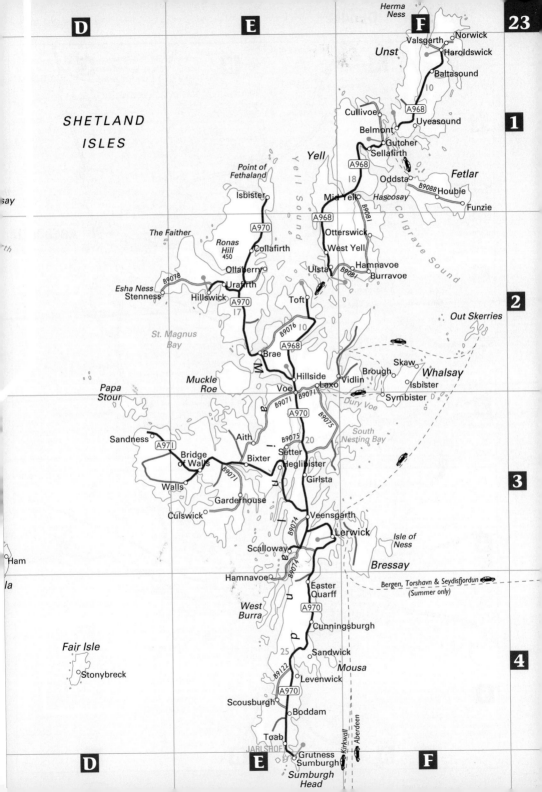

1

2

3

4

Herma
Ness

Valsgarth   Norwick
Unst   Haroldswick
Baltasound
10

A968

Cullivoe   Uyeasound
Belmont
Gutcher
Sellafirth
Yell   A968
18   Oddsta   B9088   Houbie
Mid Yell   *Fetlar*
Hascosay
Funzie

SHETLAND
ISLES

Point of
Fethaland

A968

Isbister   Otterswick
West Yell
A970   B9081
Ulsta   Hamnavoe
Burravoe

The Faither   Collafirth
*Ronas
Hill
450*   Out Skerries
Ollaberry   Toft
B9078   Urafirth   B9076   10
Esha Ness   Hillswick   A968
Stenness   17   Brae
Skaw
*St. Magnus
Bay*   Hillside   Brough
Voe   Vidlin   *Whalsay*
*Muckle
Roe*   Laxo   Isbister
*Papa
Stour*   Dury Voe   Symbister
B9071   B9071
A970   B9075
Sandness   Aith   Setter   *South
Nesting Bay*
A971   Bixter   20
Bridge   Heglibister
of Walls   B9071   Girlsta
Walls   Veensgarth
Garderhouse
Culswick   Lerwick
*Isle of
Ness*
Ham   Scalloway
Bressay
la   Hamnavoe   *Bergen, Torshavn & Seydisfjordun*
Easter   *(Summer only)*
*West
Burra*   Quarff
A970
Cunningsburgh
Fair Isle   Sandwick   *Mousa*
25
Stonybreck   B9122   Levenwick
A970
Scousburgh
Boddam
Toab
JARLSHOF   Grutness
Sumburgh
*Sumburgh
Head*

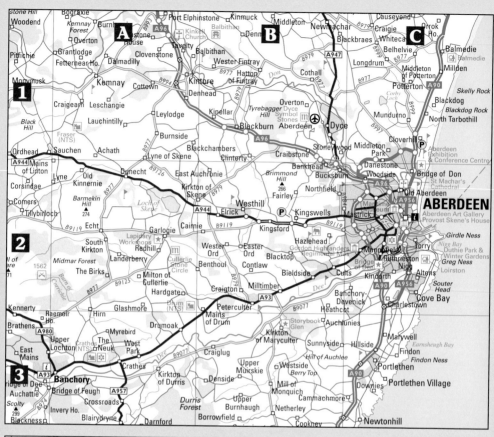

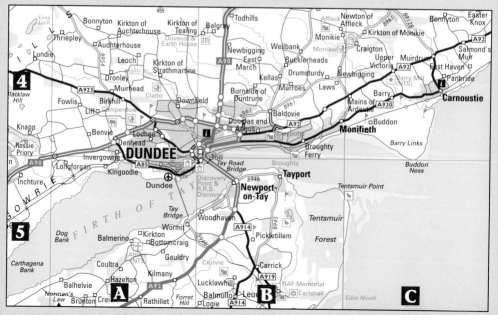

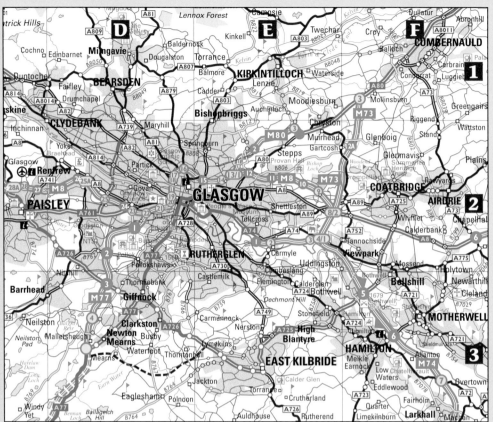

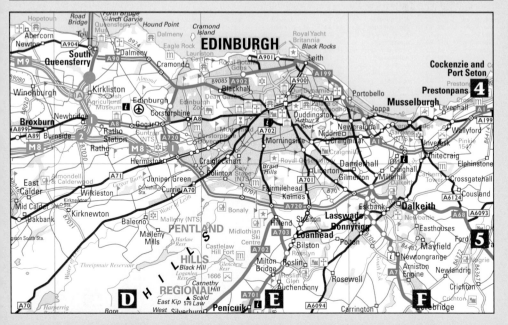

INDEX TO PLACE NAMES

Administrative Area Abbreviations

Aber.	Aberdeenshire	*E.Dun.*	East Dunbartonshire	*Ork.*	Orkney
Arg. & B.	Argyll & Bute	*Edin.*	Edinburgh	*P. & K.*	Perthshire & Kinross
Cumb.	Cumbria	*High.*	Highland	*S.Ayr.*	South Ayrshire
D. & G.	Dumfries & Galloway	*Midloth.*	Midlothian	*S.Lan.*	South Lanarkshire
Dur.	Durham	*N.Lan.*	North Lanarkshire	*Sc.Bord.*	Scottish Borders
E.Ayr.	East Ayrshire	*Northumb.*	Northumberland	*Shet.*	Shetland

Stir.	Stirling
T. & W.	Tyne & Wear
W.Dun.	West Dunbartonshire
W. Isles	Western Isles
	(Na h-Eileanan an Iar)
W. Loth.	West Lothian

Note: Index entries shown in **bold** type can be found on the urban area maps, pages 24-25

A

Abbeytown	3	E2
Aberchirder	17	D2
Aberdeen	17	F4
Aberdeen	**24**	**C2**
Aberdeen Airport	17	E4
Aberdeen Airport	**24**	**B1**
Aberdour	8	B1
Aberfeldy	12	B2
Aberfoyle	12	A4
Aberlady	8	C1
Aberlemno	13	E2
Aberlour	16	C3
Abernethy	12	C4
Aberuthven	12	C4
Abhainnsuidhe	21	D3
Abington	8	A3
Aboyne	17	D4
Abronhill	**25**	**F1**
Achadh Mòr	21	E2
Achahoish	6	C1
Acharacle	10	C2
Achath	**24**	**A1**
Achavanich	19	E2
Achfary	18	B2
Achiltibuie	18	A3
Achintee	15	D3
Achnacroish	11	D3
Achnasheen	15	E2
Achosnich	10	C2
Achriesgill	18	B2
Acomb	4	B1
Aird Asaig	21	D3
Aird of Sleat	14	B4
Airdrie	7	G2
Airdrie	**25**	**F2**
Airidh a'Bhruaich	21	E2
Airth	8	A1
Aith *Ork.*	22	C2
Aith *Shet.*	23	E3
Akeld	9	E3
Alexandria	7	E1
Alford	17	D4
Allanton *N.Lan.*	8	A2
Allanton S.Lan.	**25**	**F3**
Allendale Town	4	B2
Allenheads	4	B2
Allnabad	18	C2
Alloa	12	B4
Allonby	3	E2
Alloway	7	E3
Alness	16	A2
Alnmouth	9	F4
Alnwick	9	F4
Alston	4	A2
Altens	**24**	**C2**
Altnafeadh	11	F2
Altnaharra	18	C2
Alva	12	B4
Alves	16	B2
Alvie	16	A4
Alyth	13	D2
Amble	9	F4
Ambleside	3	F4
Amulree	12	B3
An Tairbeart (Tarbert)	21	E3
An t-òb (Leverburgh)	21	D4
Ancroft	9	E2
Ancrum	9	D3
Andreas	2	B4
Annan	3	E1
Annbank	7	E3
Annfield Plain	4	C2
Anstruther	13	E4
Aoradh	6	A3
Appleby-in-Westmorland	4	A3
Applecross	14	C3
Arbirlot	13	E3
Arbroath	13	E3

Ardchiavaig	10	B4
Arden	7	E1
Ardentinny	7	E1
Ardeonaig	12	A3
Ardersier	16	A2
Ardfern	11	D4
Ardgay	18	C4
Ardlui	11	F4
Ardlussa	6	B1
Ardmair	18	A4
Ardminish	6	B2
Ardmolich	11	D1
Ardrishaig	6	C1
Ardrossan	7	E2
Ardtalnaig	12	A3
Ardtoe	10	C2
Ardvasar	14	C4
Arinagour	10	B2
Arisaig	10	C1
Armadale	8	A1
Arnisdale	14	C4
Arniston Engine	**25**	**F5**
Arnol	21	E1
Arnprior	12	A4
Arrochar	11	F4
Ashgill	25	F3
Ashington	5	D1
Ashkirk	8	C3
Aspatria	3	E2
Attadale	15	D3
Auchallater	12	C1
Auchenblae	13	E1
Auchenbreck	6	D1
Auchencairn	3	D2
Auchencrow	9	E2
Auchendinny	**25**	**E5**
Auchindrain	11	E4
Auchinleck	7	F3
Auchinloch	**25**	**E1**
Auchlunies	**24**	**B3**
Auchmull	13	E1
Auchnagatt	17	F3
Aucholzie	13	D1
Auchterarder	12	B4
Auchterhouse	**24**	**A4**
Auchtermuchty	13	D4
Auchtertool	8	B1
Auldhouse	**25**	**E3**
Aultbea	15	D1
Aultguish Inn	15	E2
Aviemore	16	B4
Avoch	16	A2
Avonbridge	8	A1
Aycliffe	5	D3
Ayr	7	E3
Aysgarth	4	C4

B

Backaland	22	B2
Badcaul	18	A4
Badenscoth	17	E3
Badlipster	19	F2
Bàgh a' Chaisteil (Castlebay)	20	A4
Baile Ailein (Balallan)	21	E2
Baile a'Mhanaich (Balivanich)	20	A2
Baile Mhartainn	20	A1
Baile Mòr	10	B3
Bainbridge	4	B4
Balallan (Baile Ailein)	21	E2
Balbeggie	12	C3
Balbithan	**24**	**A1**
Balblair	16	A2
Baldernock	**25**	**D1**
Baldovie	**24**	**B4**
Balemartine	10	A3
Balephuil	10	A3
Balerno	**25**	**D5**

Balfour	22	B3
Balfron	7	F1
Balgown	14	B2
Balgray	13	D3
Balgray	**24**	**B4**
Balhelvie	**24**	**A5**
Balintore	16	A2
Balivanich	20	A2
(Baile a'Mhanaich)		
Ballachulish	11	E2
Ballantrae	2	A1
Ballater	13	D1
Ballaugh	2	B4
Ballingry	12	C4
Ballinluig	12	C2
Ballintuim	12	C2
Balloch N.Lan.	**25**	**F1**
Balloch *W.Dun.*	7	E1
Ballochroy	6	C2
Ballygrant	6	A2
Balmacara	14	C3
Balmaha	7	E1
Balmedie	**24**	**C1**
Balmerino	13	D3
Balmerino	**24**	**A5**
Balmore	**25**	**E1**
Balmullo	**24**	**B5**
Balnacra	15	D3
Balnahard	10	C3
Balnapaling	16	A2
Balquhidder	12	A3
Baltasound	23	F1
Balvicar	11	D4
Bamburgh	9	F3
Banchory	13	E1
Banchory	**24**	**A3**
Banchory-Devenick	**24**	**C2**
Banff	17	E2
Bankfoot	12	C3
Bankhead	**24**	**B2**
Bannockburn	8	A1
Barabhas (Barvas)	21	E1
Barassie	7	E3
Barbaraville	16	A2
Bargrennan	2	B1
Barnard Castle	4	C3
Barr	7	E4
Barrapoll	10	A3
Barrhead	7	F2
Barrhead	**25**	**D3**
Barrhill	2	B1
Barrock	19	F1
Barry	**24**	**C4**
Barvas (Barabhas)	21	E1
Bathgate	8	A1
Beadnell	9	F3
Bearsden	7	F1
Bearsden	**25**	**D1**
Beattock	8	B4
Beauly	15	F3
Bedale	5	D4
Bedlington	4	C1
Beith	7	E2
Belford	9	F3
Belhelvie	**24**	**C1**
Bellingham	4	B1
Bellshill	7	G2
Bellshill	**25**	**F3**
Belmont	23	F1
Belsay	4	C1
Benthoul	**24**	**B2**
Benvie	**24**	**A4**
Bernisdale	14	B2
Berriedale	19	E3
Berwick-upon-Tweed	9	E2
Bettyhill	18	C1
Bieldside	**24**	**B2**
Biggar	8	A3
Bilbster	19	F2
Billingham	5	D3

Billy Row	4	C2
Bilston	8	B2
Bilston	**25**	**E5**
Bimbister	22	B3
Birkhill	**24**	**A4**
Birsay	22	A2
Birtley	5	D2
Bishop Auckland	4	C3
Bishopbriggs	7	F1
Bishopbriggs	**25**	**E2**
Bishopton	7	F1
Bixter	23	E3
Blackbraes	**24**	**B1**
Blackburn *Aber.*	17	E4
Blackburn *Aber.*	**24**	**B1**
Blackburn *W.Loth.*	8	A2
Blackchambers	**24**	**A1**
Blackdog	**24**	**C1**
Blackford	12	B4
Blackhall	**25**	**E4**
Blackhall Colliery	5	D2
Blacklunans	12	C2
Blackridge	8	A1
Blacktop	**24**	**B2**
Blackwaterfoot	6	C3
Blaich	11	E1
Blair Atholl	12	B2
Blairgowrie	12	C3
Blairdryne	**24**	**A3**
Blaydon	4	C1
Blyth	5	D1
Blyth Bridge	8	B2
Boat of Garten	16	B4
Boath	15	F2
Boddam *Aber.*	17	F3
Boddam *Shet.*	23	E4
Bogniebrae	17	D3
Bograxie	**24**	**A1**
Boldon	5	D2
Boltby	5	D4
Bolton	8	C1
Bonar Bridge	18	C4
Bonawe	11	E3
Bonawe Quarries	11	E3
Bonchester Bridge	9	D4
Bo'ness	8	A1
Bonjedward	9	D3
Bonnybridge	8	A1
Bonnyrigg	8	C2
Bonnyrigg	**25**	**F5**
Bonnyton (East)	**24**	**C4**
Angus		
Bonnyton (West)	**24**	**A4**
Angus		
Bootle	3	E4
Boreland	8	B4
Boreraig	14	A2
Borgh	20	A4
Borgue *D. & G.*	2	C2
Borgue *High.*	19	E3
Borrowdale	3	F3
Borrowfield	**24**	**B3**
Borve	14	B3
Bothel	3	E2
Bothwell	**25**	**F3**
Bottomcraig	**24**	**A5**
Bournmoor	5	D2
Bow	22	B4
Bowburn	5	D2
Bowes	4	B3
Bowmore	6	A2
Bowness-on-Solway	3	E1
Bowness-on-Windermere	3	F4
Bracadale	14	A3
Braco	12	B4
Bracora	11	D1
Brae	23	E2
Braeantra	15	F1
Braehead	**25**	**D2**

Braemar	12	C1
Bragar	21	E1
Braithwaite	3	E3
Brampton	4	A2
Brandon	4	C2
Breakish	14	C4
Breanais	21	D2
Breascleit	21	E2
Brechin	13	E2
Bridge of Allan	12	B4
Bridge of Balgie	12	A2
Bridge of Cally	12	C2
Bridge of Craigisla	13	D2
Bridge of Don	17	F4
Bridge of Don	**24**	**C2**
Bridge of Dun	13	E2
Bridge of Dye	13	E1
Bridge of Earn	12	C4
Bridge of Orchy	11	F3
Bridge of Walls	23	E3
Bridge of Weir	7	E2
Bridgend *Angus*	13	E2
Bridgend (Islay)	6	A2
Arg. & B.		
Bridgend *Arg. & B.*	6	C1
(Lochgilphead)		
Bridgend *Moray*	16	C3
Brig o'Turk	12	A4
Brigham	3	E3
Brinian	22	B2
Broadford	14	C4
Brochel	14	B3
Brodick	6	D3
Brompton	5	D4
Brompton on Swale	4	C4
Brora	19	D4
Brotton	5	E3
Brough *Cumb.*	4	B3
Brough *High.*	19	E1
Brough *Shet.*	23	F2
Broughton	8	B3
Broughton in Furness	3	E4
Broughtown	22	C2
Broughty Ferry	13	E3
Broughty Ferry	**24**	**B4**
Broxburn	8	B1
Brunton	**24**	**A5**
Buchlyvie	12	A4
Buckhaven	13	D4
Buckie	17	D2
Bucklerheads	**24**	**B4**
Bucksburn	17	E4
Bucksburn	**24**	**B2**
Buddon	**24**	**C4**
Buldoo	19	E1
Bunessan	10	B4
Burgh by Sands	3	F2
Burghead	16	B2
Burness	22	C2
Burnhervie	**24**	**A1**
Burnhouse	7	E2
Burniston	5	F4
Burnmouth	9	E2
Burnopfield	4	C2
Burnside	**24**	**A1**
Burnside of Duntrune	**24**	**B4**
Burntisland	8	B1
Burravoe	23	F2
Burrelton	12	C3
Burwick	22	B4
Busby	**25**	**D3**
Buttermere	3	E3

C

Cadder	**25**	**E1**
Cairnbaan	6	C1
Cairndow	11	E4
Cairneyhill	8	A1
Caimie	**24**	**B2**

Place		
Cairnryan	2	A1
Calanais (Callanish)	21	E2
Caldbeck	3	F2
Calderbank	25	F2
Caldercruix	8	A1
Calderglen	25	E3
Caldwell	4	C3
Calfsound	22	B2
Calgary	10	B2
Callander	12	A4
Callanish (Calanais)	21	E2
Calvine	12	B2
Camasnacroise	11	D2
Cambuslang	25	E2
Cammachmore	24	C3
Campbeltown	6	C3
Camptown	9	D4
Cannich	15	E3
Canonbie	3	F1
Caolas	10	A2
Caolas Scalpaigh	21	E3
(Kyles Scalpay)		
Cappercleuch	8	B3
Capplegill	8	B4
Caputh	12	C3
Carbost	14	B3
(Loch Harport)		
High.		
Carbost	14	B3
(Loch Snizort Beag)		
High.		
Carbrain	25	F1
Cardenden	13	D4
Cardross	7	E1
Cargenbridge	3	D1
Cargill	12	C3
Carlabhagh	21	E1
(Carloway)		
Carlisle	3	F2
Carlops	8	B2
Carloway	21	E1
(Carlabhagh)		
Carluke	8	A2
Carmunnock	25	E3
Carmyle	25	E2
Carmyllie	13	E3
Carnbee	13	E4
Carnbo	12	C4
Carnoustie	13	E4
Camoustie	24	C4
Carnwath	8	A2
Carradale	6	C3
Carrbridge	16	B3
Carrick	24	B5
Carrington	25	F5
Carronbridge	8	A4
Carsaig	10	C3
Carsluith	2	C2
Carsphairn	7	F4
Carstairs	8	A2
Castle Carrock	4	A2
Castle Douglas	3	D2
Castle Kennedy	2	A2
Castlebay	20	A4
(Bàgh a' Chaisteil)		
Castlemilk	25	E3
Castleside	4	C2
Castleton	5	E4
Castletown	19	E1
Catrine	7	F3
Catterick	4	C4
Catterick Camp	4	C4
Causeyend	24	C1
Cawdor	16	A2
Ceann a'Bhàigh	20	A1
Cearsiadar	21	E2
Ceres	13	D4
Champany	8	A1
Chapelhall	25	F2
Charlestown	17	F4
Charlestown	24	C2
Chatton	9	E3
Chester-le-Street	5	D2
Chesters	9	D4
Chilton	5	D2
Chirnside	9	E2
Chopwell	4	C2
Christon Bank	9	F3
Chryston	7	G1
Chryston	25	E1
Cille Bhrighde	20	A3
Clabhach	10	A2
Clachan (Kintyre)	6	C2
Arg. & B.		
Clachan (Loch Fyne)	11	E4
Arg. & B.		
Clachan (Raasay)	14	B3
High.		
Clachan of Glendaruel	6	D1
Clachtoll	18	A3
Clackmannan	8	A1
Cladich	11	E3
Claggan	11	D2
Claonaig	6	C2
Clarkston	25	D3
Clashmore	16	A1
Clashnessie	18	A3
Cleadale	10	C1
Cleadon	5	D1
Cleat	22	B4
Cleator Moor	3	E3
Cleland	8	A2
Cleland	25	F3
Clestrain	22	A3
Clinterty	24	B1
Closeburn	8	A4
Cloughton	5	F4
Clova	13	D1
Clovenfords	8	C3
Clovenstone	24	A1
Cloverhill	24	C1
Clovullin	11	E2
Clunes	11	E1
Clydebank	7	F1
Clydebank	25	D2
Coalburn	8	A3
Coast	15	D1
Coatbridge	7	G2
Coatbridge	25	F2
Cock Bridge	16	C4
Cockburnspath	9	D1
Cockenzie &	8	C1
Port Seton		
Cockermouth	3	E3
Cockfield	4	C3
Coldingham	9	E2
Coldstream	9	E3
Colinton	25	E5
Colintraive	6	D1
Collafirth	23	E2
Collieston	17	F3
Collin	3	E1
Colmonell	2	A1
Colnabaichin	16	C4
Colquhar	8	C2
Comrie	12	B3
Condorrat	25	F1
Coniston	3	F4
Connel	11	D3
Conon Bridge	15	F2
Consett	4	C2
Contin	15	F2
Contlaw	24	B2
Cookney	24	B3
Copley	4	C3
Corbridge	4	B1
Cornhill	17	D2
Cornhill-on-Tweed	9	E3
Corpach	11	E1
Corrie	6	D2
Corsock	3	D1
Corstorphine	25	D4
Coshieville	12	B2
Cothall	24	B1
Cottown	24	A1
Coulport	7	E1
Coultra	24	A5
Cove *Arg. & B.*	4	C3
Cove *High.*	14	C1
Cove Bay	17	F4
Cove Bay	24	C2
Cowdenbeath	8	B1
Cowie	8	A1
Cowshill	4	B2
Coylton	7	E3
Coylumbridge	16	B4
Craibstone	24	B1
Craichie	13	E2
Craig	15	D3
Craigandaive	7	D1
Craigdarroch	7	F4
Craigearn	24	A1
Craigellachie	16	C3
Craigendoran	7	E1
Craighat	7	F1
Craigie	24	C1
Craiglockhart	25	E4
Craiglug	24	B3
Craigmillar	25	E4
Craignure	11	D3
Craigton *Aberdeen*	24	B2
Craigton *Angus*	24	C4
Crail	13	E4
Cramlington	5	D1
Cramond	8	B1
Cramond	25	D4
Cranshaws	9	D2
Crask Inn	18	C3
Craster	9	F3
Crathes	24	A3
Crathie	13	D1
Crawfordjohn	8	A3
Creag Ghoraidh	20	B2
(Creagorry)		
Creagorry	20	B2
(Creag Ghoraidh)		
Creetown	2	C2
Creich	24	A5
Crianlarich	11	F3
Crichton	25	F5
Crieff	12	B3
Crimond	17	F2
Crinan	11	D4
Crocketford or	3	D1
Ninemile Bar		
Cromarty	16	A2
Crook	4	C3
Crookham	9	E3
Crosbost	21	E2
Crosby Ravensworth	4	A3
Crossaig	6	C2
Crosscanonby	3	E2
Crossford *Fife*	8	B1
Crossford *S.Lan.*	8	A2
Crossgatehall	25	F5
Crossgates	8	B1
Crosshands	7	F3
Crosshill	7	E4
Crosshouse	7	E3
Crossmichael	2	C1
Crossroads	24	A3
Croy *High.*	16	A3
Croy *N.Lan.*	7	G1
Croy *N.Lan.*	25	F1
Cruden Bay	17	F3
Crùlabhig	21	E2
Crutherland	25	E3
Culbokie	15	F2
Culdrain	17	D3
Cullen	17	D2
Cullicudden	16	A2
Cullipool	11	D4
Cullivoe	23	F1
Culnacraig	18	A4
Culnaknock	14	B2
Culross	8	A1
Culswick	23	E3
Cults	17	E4
Cults	24	B2
Cumbernauld	7	G1
Cumbernauld	25	F1
Cuminestown	17	E2
Cumnock	7	F3
Cunningsburgh	23	E4
Cupar	13	D4
Currie	25	D5

D

Place		
Dacre	3	F3
Dail Bho Thuath	21	F1
(North Dell)		
Dailly	7	E4
Dairsie	13	D4
Dalabrog	20	A3
Dalbeattie	3	D2
Dalgety Bay	8	B1
Dalkeith	8	C1
Dalkeith	25	F5
Dallas	16	B2
Dalmadilly	24	A1
Dalmally	11	E3
Dalmellington	7	F4
Dalmeny	25	D4
Dalnacraig	16	A2
Dalry	7	E2
Dalrymple	7	E4
Dalserf	25	F3
Dalston	3	F2
Dalwhinnie	12	A1
Danby	5	E4
Danderhall	25	F5
Danestone	24	C1
Darlington	5	D3
Darnford	24	A3
Darra	17	E3
Darvel	7	F3
Dava	16	B3
Daviot	16	A3
Dearham	3	E3
Dechmont	8	A1
Denhead *Aber.*	24	A1
Denhead *Dundee*	24	A4
Denholm	9	D3
Denmill	24	B1
Denny	8	A1
Denside	24	B3
Dervaig	10	C2
Dhoon	2	B4
Dingwall	15	F2
Dinnet	17	D4
Dippen	6	C3
Dirleton	8	C1
Distington	3	E3
Dochgarroch	15	F3
Doddington	9	E3
Dollar	12	B4
Dolphinton	8	B2
Dores	15	F3
Dornie	15	D3
Dornoch	16	A1
Dougalston	25	D1
Dougarie	6	C3
Douglas	8	A3
Douglas	24	B4
& Angus		
Douglastown	13	D2
Dounby	22	A3
Doune	12	B4
Dounreay	19	E1
Dowally	12	C2
Downfield	24	A4
Downies	24	C3
Dreghorn	7	E3
Drem	8	C1
Drimnin	10	C2
Drongan	7	F3
Dronley	24	A4
Druimdrishaig	6	C1
Drumbeg	18	A3
Drumchapel	25	D1
Drumclog	7	F3
Drumlithie	13	F1
Drummore	2	A2
Drumnadrochit	15	F3
Drumoak	24	A3
Drumsturdy	24	B4
Drymen	7	F1
Duddingston	25	E4
Duddo	9	E2
Dufftown	16	C3
Duirinish	14	C3
Dullatur	25	F1
Dulnain Bridge	16	B3
Dumbarton	7	E1
Dumfries	3	D1
Dunbar	9	D1
Dunbeath	19	E3
Dunblane	12	B4
Dundee	13	D3
Dundee	24	B4
Dundee Airport	24	A5
Dundonald	7	E3
Dundreggan	15	E4
Dundrennan	3	D2
Dunecht	17	E4
Dunecht	24	A2
Dunfermline	8	B1
Dunkeld	12	C3
Dunlop	7	E2
Dunnet	19	E1
Dunning	12	C4
Dunoon	7	E1
Dunragit	2	A2
Duns	9	D2
Dunscore	3	D1
Dunure	7	E3
Dunvegan	14	A3
Durham	5	D2
Durness	18	B1
Dyce	17	E4
Dyce	24	B1
Dyke	16	B2
Dykehead	13	D2

E

Place		
Eaglescliffe	5	D3
Eaglesfield	3	E1
Eaglesham	7	F2
Eaglesham	25	D3
Earlston	9	D3
Earsairidh	20	A4
Easdale	11	D4
Easington	5	D2
Easington Colliery	5	D2
East Auchronie	24	B2
East Calder	8	B1
East Haven	13	E3
East Haven	24	C4
East Kilbride	7	F2
East Kilbride	25	E3
East Linton	9	D1
East March	24	B4
East Wemyss	13	D4
Easter Knox	24	C4
Easter Lednathie	13	D2
Easter Ord	24	B2
Easter Quarff	23	E4
Eastgate	4	B2
Easthouses	25	F5
Eastriggs	3	F1
Ecclaw	9	D1
Ecclefechan	3	E1
Eccles	9	D2
Echt	17	E4
Echt	24	A2
Eckford	9	D3
Edderton	16	A1
Eddleston	8	B2
Eddlewood	25	F3
Edinbarnet	25	D1
Edinburgh	8	B1
Edinburgh	25	E4
Edinburgh Airport	8	B1
Edinburgh Airport	25	D4
Edingham	9	F4
Edmundbyers	4	C2
Edzell	13	E2
Egglescliffe	5	D3
Eglingham	9	F3
Egremont	3	E3
Egton	5	F4
Einacleit	21	D2
Elgin	16	C2
Elgol	14	B4
Elie	13	E4
Ellingham	9	F3
Ellington	9	F4
Ellon	17	F3
Elphin	18	B3
Elphinstone	25	F4
Elrick	24	B2
Elsdon	9	E4
Elsrickle	8	B2
Elvanfoot	8	A3
Embleton	9	F3
Enterkinfoot	8	A4
Eoropaidh	21	F1
Eriboll	18	B2
Errogie	15	F4
Errol	13	D3
Esh Winning	4	C2
Eskbank	25	E4
Eskdalemuir	8	B4
Eston	5	E3
Etteridge	12	A1
Ettrick	8	B4
Ettrickbridge	8	C3
Evanton	15	F2
Eyemouth	9	E2

F

Place		
Faifley	25	D1
Fairholm	25	F3
Fairley	24	B2
Fairlie	7	E2
Fairmilehead	25	E5
Falkirk	8	A1
Falkland	13	D4
Fallin	8	A1
Falstone	4	A1
Farr	16	A3
Fauldhouse	8	A2
Fearnmore	14	C2
Felling	5	D1
Felton	9	F4
Fenwick *E.Ayr.*	7	F2
Fenwick	9	F2
Northumb.		

Name	Pg	Grid
Feochaig	6	C4
Feolin Ferry	6	B1
Fern	13	E2
Ferness	16	B3
Ferryden	13	E2
Ferryhill	5	D3
Feshiebridge	16	A4
Fettercairn	13	E1
Fetternear House	24	A1
Finavon	13	E2
Findhorn	16	B2
Findochty	17	D2
Findon	24	C3
Finnygaud	17	D2
Finstown	22	B3
Fintry	7	F1
Fionnphort	10	B3
Fishburn	5	D3
Fishnish	10	C3
Fiunary	10	C2
Flemington	25	E3
Flimby	3	E3
Flodden	9	E3
Fochabers	16	C2
Ford *Arg. & B.*	11	D4
Ford *Midloth.*	25	F5
Ford *Northumb.*	9	E3
Fordoun	13	F1
Fordyce	17	D2
Forfar	13	D2
Forgandenny	12	C3
Forgie	16	C2
Forres	16	B2
Forsinard	19	D2
Fort Augustus	15	E4
Fort William	11	E1
Forth	8	A2
Fortingall	12	B2
Fortrose	16	A2
Foulden	9	E2
Fowlis	24	A4
Foyers	15	F4
Fraserburgh	17	F2
Freswick	19	F1
Freuchie	13	D4
Friockheim	13	E2
Frizington	3	E3
Funzie	23	F1
Furnace	11	E4
Fyvie	17	E3

G

Name	Pg	Grid
Gainford	4	C3
Gairloch	14	C1
Galashiels	8	C3
Galmisdale	10	C1
Galston	7	F3
Gardenstown	17	E2
Garderhouse	23	E3
Garelochhead	7	E1
Garlieston	2	C2
Garlogie	24	A2
Garsdale Head	4	B4
Gartcosh	25	E2
Gartocharn	7	F1
Garvald	9	D1
Garvamore	12	A1
Garvard	15	F2
Garve	15	F2
Gatehouse of Fleet	2	C2
Gateshead	5	D2
Gauldry	24	A5
Gawthrop	4	A4
Gearraidh na h-Aibhne	21	E2
Giffnock	7	F2
Giffnock	25	D3
Gifford	8	C1
Gillamoor	5	E4
Gilling West	4	C4
Gilmerton *Edin.*	25	E5
Gilmerton *P. & K.*	12	B3
Gilsland	4	A1
Gilston	8	C2
Girlsta	23	E3
Girvan	7	E4
Glamis	13	D2
Glanton	9	E3
Glasgow	7	F2
Glasgow	25	D2
Glasgow Airport	7	F2
Glasgow Prestwick International Airport	7	F2
Glashmore	24	A2
Glassford	7	G2
Glenbarr	6	C3
Glenbeg	10	C2
Glenboig	25	F2
Glenborrodale	10	C2
Glenbreck	8	B3
Glenbrittle	14	B4
Glencaple	3	E1
Glencarse	12	C3
Glencoe	11	E2
Gleneagles	12	B4
Glenegedale	6	A2
Glenelg	14	C4
Glenfarg	12	C4
Glenfinnan	11	D1
Glengarnock	7	E2
Glenkindie	17	D4
Glenluce	2	A2
Glenmavis	25	F2
Glenrothes	13	D4
Gogar	25	D4
Golspie	19	D4
Gordon	9	D2
Gorebridge	8	C2
Gorebridge	25	F5
Gosforth *Cumb.*	3	E4
Gosforth *T. & W.*	4	C1
Gourdon	13	F2
Govan	25	D2
Grabhair	21	E2
Grandtully	12	B2
Grangemouth	8	A1
Grantlodge	24	A1
Grantown-on-Spey	16	B3
Grantshouse	9	D2
Grasmere	3	F4
Grayrigg	4	A4
Great Ayton	5	E3
Great Broughton	5	E4
Great Clifton	3	E3
Great Salkeld	4	A2
Greengairs	7	G1
Greengairs	25	F1
Greenhead	4	A1
Greenigo	22	B3
Greenlaw	9	D2
Greenloaning	12	B4
Greenock	7	E1
Gress (Griais)	21	F1
Gretna	3	F1
Greystoke	3	F3
Griais (Gress)	21	F1
Gritley	22	B3
Grizebeck	3	E4
Grudie	15	E2
Grutness	23	E4
Guide Post	4	C1
Guildtown	12	C3
Guisborough	5	E3
Gullane	8	C1
Gutcher	23	F1

Name	Pg	Grid
Hebburn	5	D1
Heglibister	23	E3
Helensburgh	7	E1
Helmsdale	19	E3
Helmsley	5	E4
Heriot	8	C2
Hermiston	25	D4
Herston	22	B4
Hetton-le-Hole	5	D2
Hexham	4	B1
High Blantyre	7	G2
High Blantyre	25	E3
High Etherley	4	C3
High Hawsker	5	F4
High Hesket	3	F2
High Lorton	3	E3
Hill End	12	C4
Hill of Fearn	16	A1
Hillend	25	E5
Hillside *Aber.*	24	C3
Hillside *Angus*	13	E2
Hillside *Shet.*	23	E2
Hillswick	23	E2
Hinderwell	5	F3
Him	24	A2
Hollybush	7	E3
Holytown	25	F2
Holywood	3	D1
Hopeman	16	B2
Horden	5	D2
Houbie	23	F1
Houghton le Spring	5	D2
Houndslow	9	D2
Houston	7	E2
Houton	22	B3
Howwood	7	F2
Huisinis	21	D3
Humbie	8	C2
Hunter's Quay	7	E1
Huntly	17	D3
Hurlford	7	F3
Hurworth-on-Tees	5	D3
Hutton Rudby	5	D4

I

Name	Pg	Grid
Idrigil	14	B2
Inchbare	13	E2
Inchnadamph	18	B3
Inchture	13	D3
Ingleton	4	C3
Innellan	7	D1
Innerleithen	8	C3
Insch	17	D3
Inveralligin	14	C2
Inverallochy	17	F2
Inveraray	11	E4
Inverarity	13	D3
Inverarnan	11	F4
Inverbervie	13	F1
Invercassley	18	C4
Invercharnan	11	E2
Inveresk	25	F4
Inverey	12	C1
Invergarry	15	E4
Invergordon	16	A2
Invergowrie	24	A4
Inverinan	11	E4
Inverkeilor	13	E2
Inverkeithing	8	B1
Inverkirkaig	18	A3
Inverlael	15	E1
Invermoriston	15	F4
Inverneil	7	D1
Inverness	16	A3
Inverness Airport	16	A3
Invernoaden	11	E4
Inverurie	17	E4
Irvine	7	E3
Isbister (Mainland) *Shet.*	23	E1
Isbister (Whalsay) *Shet.*	23	F2
Isle of Whithorn	2	C2

J

Name	Pg	Grid
Jackton	25	D3
Jarrow	5	D1
Jedburgh	9	D3
Jemimaville	16	A2
John o' Groats	19	F1
Johnstone	7	F2
Johnstonebridge	8	B4
Joppa	25	F4

Name	Pg	Grid
Juniper Green	25	D5

K

Name	Pg	Grid
Kaimes	25	E5
Kames	6	D1
Keillmore	6	C1
Keiss	19	F1
Keith	17	D2
Kellas *Angus*	13	D3
Kellas *Angus*	24	B4
Kellas *Moray*	16	C2
Kelso	9	D3
Kelty	12	C4
Kemnay	17	E4
Kemnay	24	A1
Kendal	4	A4
Kenmore	12	B2
Kennacraig	6	C2
Kennethmont	17	D3
Kennoway	13	D4
Kensaleyre	14	B2
Kentallen	11	E2
Keswick	3	F3
Kettletoft	22	C2
Kielder	9	D4
Kilberry	6	C2
Kilbirnie	7	E2
Kilcadzow	8	A2
Kilchattan	10	B4
Kilchenzie	6	C3
Kilchiaran	6	A3
Kilchoan	10	C2
Kilchoman	6	A3
Kilchrenan	11	E3
Kilconquhar	13	E4
Kilcreggan	7	E1
Kildonan Lodge	19	D3
Kildrummy	17	D4
Kilfinan	6	D1
Kilham	9	E3
Killean	6	C2
Killearn	7	F1
Killichonan	12	A2
Killiecrankie	12	B2
Killin	12	A3
Killingworth	5	D1
Killundine	10	C2
Kilmacolm	7	E1
Kilmalieu	11	D2
Kilmaluag	14	B2
Kilmany	24	A5
Kilmarnock	7	F3
Kilmartin	11	D4
Kilmaurs	7	E2
Kilmelford	11	D4
Kilmory *Arg. & B.*	6	C1
Kilmory (Rum) *High.*	10	B2
Kilninian	10	B2
Kilninver	11	D3
Kiloran	10	B4
Kilrenny	13	E4
Kilsyth	7	G1
Kilwinning	7	E2
Kinbrace	19	D3
Kincardine	8	A1
Kincardine O'Neil	17	D4
Kincorth	24	C2
Kincraig	16	A4
Kinellar	24	B1
Kingarth	7	D2
Kinghorn	8	B1
Kinglassie	13	D4
Kingoodie	24	A5
Kingsbarns	13	E4
Kingsford	24	B2
Kingshouse	12	A3
Kingston	16	C2
Kingswells	24	B2
Kingussie	16	A4
Kinkell	25	E1
Kinloch	14	B4
Kinloch Hourn	15	D4
Kinloch Rannoch	12	A2
Kinlochard	12	A4
Kinlochbervie	18	B2
Kinlocheil	11	E1
Kinlochewe	15	D2
Kinlochleven	11	E2
Kinloss	16	B2
Kinmuck	24	B1
Kinross	12	C4
Kintore	17	E4
Kintore	24	A1
Kintour	6	B2

Name	Pg	Grid
Kintra	6	A2
Kippen	12	A4
Kirk Michael	8	B4
Kirk Yetholm	9	E3
Kirkbean	3	D2
Kirkbride	3	E2
Kirkby Stephen	8	B4
Kirkbymoorside	5	E4
Kirkcaldy	8	B1
Kirkcolm	2	A1
Kirkconnel	7	G4
Kirkcowan	2	B2
Kirkcudbright	2	C2
Kirkinner	2	B2
Kirkintilloch	7	F1
Kirkintilloch	25	E1
Kirkliston	8	B1
Kirkliston	25	D4
Kirkmichael *P. & K.*	12	C2
Kirkmichael *S.Ayr.*	7	E4
Kirkmuirhill	8	A3
Kirknewton *Northumb.*	9	E3
Kirknewton *W.Loth.*	8	B1
Kirknewton *W.Loth.*	25	D5
Kirkoswald *Cumb.*	4	A2
Kirkoswald *S.Ayr.*	7	E4
Kirkpatrick Durham	3	D1
Kirkpatrick-Fleming	3	F1
Kirkton *Arg. & B.*	11	D4
Kirkton *Fife*	24	A5
Kirkton of Auchterhouse	24	A4
Kirkton of Culsalmond	17	D3
Kirkton of Durris	13	F1
Kirkton of Durris	24	A3
Kirkton of Glenisla	13	D2
Kirkton of Kingoldrum	13	D2
Kirkton of Maryculter	24	B3
Kirkton of Menmuir	13	E2
Kirkton of Monikie	24	C4
Kirkton of Skene	17	E4
Kirkton of Skene	24	B2
Kirkton of Strathmartine	24	A4
Kirkton of Tealing	24	B4
Kirktown of Auchterless	17	E3
Kirktown of Deskford	17	D2
Kirkwall	22	B3
Kirriemuir	13	D2
Knayton	5	D4
Knock	10	C3
Knockandhu	16	C4
Kyle of Lochalsh	14	C3
Kyleakin	14	C3
Kylerhea	14	C4
Kyles Scalpay (Caolas Scalpaigh)	21	E3
Kylestrome	18	B2

L

Name	Pg	Grid
Ladybank	13	D4
Ladykirk	9	E2
Ladysford	17	E2
Lagg	6	D3
Laggan (Invergarry) *High.*	11	F1
Laggan (Newtonmore) *High.*	12	A1
Lagganulva	10	C3
Laide	15	D1
Lairg	18	C4
Lamlash	6	D3
Lanark	7	G2
Lanchester	4	C2
Landerberry	24	A2
Langholm	3	F1
Langwathby	4	A2
Larbert	8	A1
Largoward	13	D4
Largs	7	E2
Larkhall	7	G2
Larkhall	25	F3
Lasswade	25	F5
Latheron	19	E3
Latheronwheel	19	E3
Lauchintilly	24	A1
Lauder	8	C3
Laurencekirk	13	E2

Name	Page	Grid
Laurieston	2	C1
Law	8	A2
Lawers	12	A3
Laws	**24**	**B4**
Laxey	2	B4
Laxford Bridge	18	B2
Laxo	23	E2
Lazonby	4	A2
Leadburn	8	B2
Leadgate	4	C2
Leadhills	8	A3
Leckmelm	15	E1
Ledaig	11	D3
Ledmore	18	B3
Leeming	5	D4
Leith	8	B1
Leith	**25**	**E4**
Lennoxtown	7	F1
Lenzie	**25**	**E1**
Leoch	**24**	**A4**
Lerwick	23	E3
Lesbury	9	F4
Leschangie	**24**	**A1**
Leslie	13	D4
Lesmahagow	8	A3
Leswalt	2	A1
Leuchars	13	D3
Leuchars	**24**	**B5**
Leumrabhagh	21	E3
Leven	13	D4
Levenhall	**25**	**F4**
Levenwick	23	E4
Leverburgh (An t-òb)	21	D4
Leyburn	4	C4
Leylodge	**24**	**A1**
Lhanbryde	16	C2
Libberton	8	A2
Liberton	**25**	**E5**
Liff	**24**	**A4**
Lilliesleaf	8	C3
Limekilnburn	**25**	**F3**
Limekilns	8	B1
Lindores	13	D4
Linksness	22	A3
Linlithgow	8	A1
Linsidemore	15	F1
Littlemill *E.Ayr.*	7	F3
Littlemill *High.*	16	B2
Livingston	8	B1
Loanhead	8	B2
Loanhead	**25**	**E5**
Loans	7	E3
Loch Baghasdail (Lochboisdale)	20	B3
Loch na Madadh (Lochmaddy)	20	B1
Loch Sgioport	20	B2
Lochailort	11	D1
Lochaline	10	C3
Lochans	2	A2
Locharbriggs	3	E1
Lochawe	11	E3
Lochboisdale (Loch Baghasdail)	20	B3
Lochcarron	15	D2
Lochdon	11	D3
Lochearnhead	12	A3
Lochee	**24**	**A4**
Lochend	15	F3
Lochgelly	12	C4
Lochgilphead	6	C1
Lochgoilhead	11	F4
Lochinver	18	A3
Lochmaben	3	E1
Lochmaddy (Loch na Madadh)	20	B1
Lochranza	6	D2
Lochwinnoch	7	E2
Lockerbie	3	E1
Lockton	5	F4
Loftus	5	E3
Logan	7	F3
Logie	**24**	**B5**
Longbenton	5	D1
Longdrum	**24**	**C1**
Longforgan	13	D3
Longforgan	**24**	**A5**
Longframlington	9	F4
Longhope	22	A4
Longhorsley	9	F4
Longhoughton	9	F3
Longmanhill	17	E2
Longmorn	16	C2
Longniddry	8	C1
Longside	17	F3
Longtown	3	F1
Lossiemouth	16	C2
Loth	22	C2
Lothmore	19	E3
Low Waters	**25**	**F3**
Lower Diabaig	14	C2
Lower Killeyan	6	A4
Loweswater	4	A3
Lowick	9	E3
Lucklawhill	**24**	**B5**
Ludag	20	A3
Luggiebank	**25**	**F1**
Luib	14	B3
Lumphanan	17	D4
Luncarty	12	C3
Lundin Links	13	D4
Luss	7	E1
Lusta	14	A2
Lybster	19	F2
Lymekilns	**25**	**E3**
Lyne	**24**	**A2**
Lyne of Skene	17	E4
Lyne of Skene	**24**	**A1**
Lynemore	16	B3
Lynemouth	9	F4
Lyness	22	A4

M

Name	Page	Grid
Macduff	17	E2
Machan	**25**	**F3**
Macharioch	6	C4
Machrihanish	6	B3
Macmerry	8	C1
Maidens	7	E4
Mains of Ardestie	**24**	**C4**
Mains of Drum	**24**	**B2**
Mains of Linton	**24**	**A2**
Mallaig	10	C1
Malleny Mills	**25**	**D5**
Malletsheugh	**25**	**D3**
Mannofield	**24**	**C2**
Markinch	13	D4
Marske-by-the-Sea	5	E3
Marybank	15	F2
Maryhill	**25**	**D2**
Marykirk	13	E2
Marypark	16	C3
Maryport	3	E2
Marywell (Deeside) *Aber.*	13	E1
Marywell (Portlethen) *Aber.*	**24**	**C3**
Mastrick	**24**	**B2**
Mauchline	7	F3
Maud	17	F3
Maughold	2	C4
Maybole	7	E4
Mayfield	**25**	**F5**
Mealsgate	3	E2
Mearns	**25**	**D3**
Meigle	13	D3
Meikle Earnock	**25**	**F3**
Meikle Kilmory	7	D2
Meikleour	12	C3
Melmerby	4	A2
Melrose	8	C3
Melsonby	4	C4
Melvaig	14	C1
Melvich	19	D1
Memsie	17	F2
Menstrie	12	B4
Methlick	17	E3
Methven	12	C3
Mey	19	F1
Miabhig (Miavaig)	21	D2
Miavaig (Miabhig)	21	D2
Mickleton	4	B3
Mid Ardlaw	17	F2
Mid Yell	23	F1
Midbea	22	B2
Middleham	4	C4
Middlesbrough	5	D3
Middleton	**24**	**B1**
Middleton of Potterton	**24**	**C1**
Middleton Park	**24**	**C1**
Middleton-in-Teesdale	4	B3
Midlem	8	C3
Milfield	9	E3
Mill of Monquich	**24**	**B3**
Millden	**24**	**B3**
Millerhill	**25**	**F5**
Millhouse	6	D1
Millport	7	D2
Milltimber	**24**	**B2**
Milltown of Rothiemay	17	D3
Milnathort	12	C4
Milngavie	7	F1
Milngavie	**25**	**D1**
Milovaig	14	A2
Milton *High.*	15	F3
Milton *P. & K.*	12	B3
Milton Bridge	**25**	**E5**
Milton of Campsie	7	F1
Milton of Campsie	**25**	**E1**
Milton of Cullerlie	**24**	**A2**
Minard	11	E4
Minnigaff	2	B1
Mintlaw	17	F3
Moffat	8	B4
Mollinsburn	**25**	**F1**
Moniaive	7	G4
Monifieth	13	E3
Monifieth	**24**	**B4**
Monikie	**24**	**B4**
Monimail	13	D4
Monreith	2	B2
Montrose	13	E2
Moodiesburn	**25**	**E1**
Morar	10	C1
Morebattle	9	D3
Morenish	12	A3
Moresby	3	E3
Morningside	**25**	**E4**
Morpeth	4	C1
Moscow	7	F3
Mossat	17	D4
Mossblown	7	E3
Mossend	**25**	**F2**
Mosstodloch	16	C2
Motherwell	7	G2
Motherwell	**25**	**F3**
Mountbenger	8	C3
Moy	16	A3
Muchalls	13	F1
Muir of Fowlis	17	D4
Muir of Ord	15	F2
Muirdrum	13	E3
Muirdrum	**24**	**C4**
Muirhead *Angus*	13	D3
Muirhead *Angus*	**24**	**A4**
Muirhead *N.Lan.*	**25**	**E2**
Muirkirk	7	G3
Mulben	16	C2
Mundurno	**24**	**C1**
Munlochy	16	A2
Murroes	**24**	**B4**
Murton	5	D2
Musselburgh	8	C1
Musselburgh	**25**	**F4**
Muthill	12	B4
Mybster	19	E2
Myrebird	**24**	**A3**

N

Name	Page	Grid
Nairn	16	A2
Nateby	4	B4
Near Sawrey	3	F4
Neilston	7	F2
Nenthead	4	B2
Nerston	**25**	**E3**
Netherley	13	F1
Netherley	**24**	**B3**
Netherton	9	E4
Nethy Bridge	16	B4
New Abbey	3	D1
New Aberdour	17	E2
New Byth	17	E2
New Cumnock	7	F4
New Deer	17	E3
New Galloway	2	C1
New Leeds	17	F2
New Luce	2	A1
New Pitsligo	17	E2
Newarthill	**25**	**F3**
Newbiggin-by-the-Sea	5	D1
Newbiggin (East) *Angus*	**24**	**B4**
Newbiggin (West) *Angus*	**24**	**B4**
Newbigging *S. Lan.*	8	A2
Newbridge	**25**	**D4**
Newburgh *Aber.*	17	F3
Newburgh *Fife*	13	D4
Newburn	4	C1
Newby Bridge	3	F4
Newcastle International Airport	4	C1
Newcastle upon Tyne	4	C1
Newcastleton	3	F1
Newcraighall	**25**	**F4**
Newlandrig	**25**	**F5**
Newmachar	17	E4
Newmachar	**24**	**B1**
Newmains	8	A2
Newmarket	21	F2
Newmill	17	D2
Newmilns	7	F3
Newport	19	E3
Newport-on-Tay	13	D3
Newport-on-Tay	**24**	**B5**
Newton	11	E4
Newton Aycliffe	5	D3
Newton Mearns	7	F2
Newton Mearns	**25**	**D3**
Newton of Affleck	**24**	**B4**
Newton Stewart	2	B1
Newtongrange	**25**	**F5**
Newtonhill	13	F1
Newtonhill	**24**	**C3**
Newtonmore	16	A4
Newtown St. Boswells	9	D3
Newtyle	13	D3
Niddrie	**25**	**E4**
Nigg	**25**	**D3**
Ninemile Bar or Crocketford	3	D1
Nisbet	9	D3
Nitshill	**25**	**D2**
Norham	9	E2
North Ballachulish	11	E2
North Berwick	8	C1
North Cowton	5	D4
North Dell (Dail Bho Thuath)	21	F1
North Kessock	16	A3
North Middleton	8	C2
North Queensferry	8	B1
North Shields	5	D1
North Sunderland	9	F3
North Tarbothill	**24**	**C1**
Northallerton	5	D4
Northfield	**24**	**B2**
Northton (Taobh Tuath)	21	D3
Norwich	23	F1

O

Name	Page	Grid
Oakley	8	A1
Oban	11	D3
Ochiltree	7	F3
Ockle	10	C2
Oddsta	23	F1
Old Aberdeen	**24**	**C2**
Old Craighall	**25**	**F4**
Old Dailly	7	E4
Old Kinnernie	**24**	**A2**
Oldmeldrum	17	E3
Olgrinmore	19	E2
Ollaberry	23	E2
Onich	11	E2
Ormiston	8	C1
Orrok House	**24**	**C1**
Orton	4	A4
Oskaig	14	B3
Otter Ferry	6	D1
Otterburn	9	E4
Otterswick	23	F2
Overbister	22	C2
Overton *Aberdeen*	**24**	**B1**
Overton *Aber.*	**24**	**A1**
Overtown	8	A2
Oxnam	9	D3
Oxton	8	C2
Oykel Bridge	15	F1

P

Name	Page	Grid
Paisley	7	F2
Palnackie	3	D2
Panbride	**24**	**C4**
Parkgate	3	E1
Partick	**25**	**D2**
Parton	3	D3
Path of Condie	12	C4
Pathhead	**25**	**F5**
Patna	7	E4
Patterdale	3	F3
Paxton	9	E2
Peebles	8	B3
Peel	2	B4
Pegswood	4	C1
Peinchorran	14	B3
Pencaitland	8	C1
Penicuik	8	B2
Penicuik	**25**	**E5**
Peninver	6	C3
Pennyghael	10	C3
Penpont	8	A4
Penrith	4	A3
Perth	12	C3
Peterculter	17	E4
Peterculter	**24**	**B2**
Peterhead	17	F3
Peterlee	5	D2
Pickering	5	F4
Pickletillem	**24**	**B5**
Pierowall	22	B2
Pinwherry	2	A1
Pirnmill	6	C2
Pitagowan	12	B2
Pitlochry	12	B2
Pitmedden	17	E3
Pitscottie	13	D4
Pittentrail	19	D4
Pittenweem	13	E4
Plains	**25**	**F2**
Plean	8	A1
Polbeth	8	A2
Polloch	11	D2
Pollokshaws	**25**	**D2**
Polmont	8	A1
Polnoon	**25**	**D3**
Polton	**25**	**E5**
Polwarth	9	D2
Ponteland	4	C1
Poolewe	14	C1
Pooley Bridge	3	F3
Port Appin	11	D3
Port Askaig	6	B1
Port Bannatyne	7	D2
Port Driseach	6	D1
Port Ellen	6	A2
Port Elphinstone	**24**	**A1**
Port Glasgow	7	E1
Port Henderson	14	C2
Port Logan	2	A2
Port nan Giùran (Portnaguran)	21	F2
Port nan Long	20	B1
Port Ness (Port Nis)	21	F1
Port Nis (Port Ness)	21	F1
Port of Menteith	12	A4
Port William	2	B2
Portencross	7	E2
Portknockie	17	D2
Portlethen	13	F1
Portlethen	**24**	**C3**
Portlethen Village	**24**	**C3**
Portmahomack	16	B1
Portnacon	18	B1
Portnacroish	11	D2
Portnaguran (Port nan Giùran)	21	F2
Portnahaven	6	A2
Portnalong	14	A3
Portobello	**25**	**F4**
Portpatrick	2	A2
Portree	14	B3
Portsoy	17	D2
Potterton	**24**	**C1**
Powburn	9	F3
Powmill	12	C4
Preston	9	D2
Prestonpans	8	C1
Prestonpans	**25**	**F4**
Prestwick	7	E3
Prestwick (Glasgow) International Airport	7	E3
Prudhoe	4	C2

Q

Name	Page	Grid
Quarter	**25**	**F3**

R

Name	Page	Grid
Rafford	16	B2
Rait	13	D3
Ramsey	2	B4
Rathillet	13	D3
Rathillet	**24**	**A5**

Name	Page	Grid
Ratho	8	B1
Ratho	**25**	**D4**
Ratho Station	**25**	**D4**
Rattray	12	C3
Ravenglass	3	E4
Rawyards	**25**	**F2**
Reay	19	D1
Red Point	14	C2
Redcar	5	E3
Redcastle	15	F3
Redford	13	E3
Redhill	**24**	**A2**
Reiss	19	F2
Renfrew	7	F1
Renfrew	**25**	**D2**
Rennington	9	F3
Rescobie	13	E2
Reston	9	E2
Rhiconich	18	B2
Rhu	7	E1
Rhynie	17	D3
Richmond	4	C4
Rickarton	13	F1
Riding Mill	4	C2
Riggend	**25**	**F2**
Rigside	8	A3
Ringford	2	C2
Roadside	19	E1
Roadside of Kinneff	13	F1
Roberton Sc.Bord.	8	C4
Roberton S.Lan.	8	A3
Robin Hood's Bay	5	F4
Rochester	9	E4
Rockcliffe	3	D2
Rodel (Roghadal)	21	D4
Rogart	19	D4
Roghadal (Rodel)	21	D4
Romannobridge	8	B2
Rosedale Abbey	5	E4
Rosehearty	17	F2
Rosemarkie	16	A2
Rosewell	8	B2
Rosewell	**25**	**E5**
Roshven	11	D1
Roskhill	14	A3
Roslin	8	B2
Roslin	**25**	**E5**
Rothbury	9	E4
Rothes	16	C3
Rothesay	7	D2
Rothiesholm	22	C3
Rowlands Gill	4	C2
Roybridge	11	F1
Rutherend	**25**	**E3**
Rutherglen	7	F2
Rutherglen	**25**	**E2**
Ruthrieston	**24**	**C2**

S

Name	Page	Grid
Sacriston	4	C2
Saddell	6	C3
Saighdinis	20	B1
St. Abbs	9	E1
St. Andrews	13	E4
St. Bees	3	D3
St. Combs	17	F2
St. Cyrus	13	F2
St. Fergus	17	F2
St. Fillans	12	A3
St. John's Chapel	4	B2
St. John's Town of Dalry	2	C1
St. Margaret's Hope	22	B4
St. Mary's	22	B3
St. Monans	13	E4
Salen Arg. & B.	10	C3
Salen High.	11	D2
Saline	8	A1
Salmond's Muir	**24**	**C4**
Salsburgh	8	A2
Saltburn-by-the-Sea	5	E3
Saltcoats	7	E2
Sanaigmore	6	A3
Sandgarth	22	B3
Sandhead	2	A2
Sandness	23	D3
Sandsend	5	F3
Sandwick	23	E4
Sandygate	2	B4
Sanquhar	7	G4
Satley	4	C2
Scalasaig	10	B4
Scalby	5	F4
Scalloway	23	E3
Scapa	22	B3
Scarborough	5	F4
Scarinish	10	A3
Scone	12	C3
Sconser	14	B3
Scorton	4	C4
Scotch Corner	4	C4
Scotton	4	C4
Scourie	18	A2
Scousburgh	23	E4
Scrabster	19	E1
Scremerston	9	E2
Seaham	5	D2
Seahouses	9	F3
Seamill	7	E2
Seascale	3	E4
Seaton	3	E3
Seaton Delaval	5	D1
Seaton Sluice	5	D1
Sedbergh	4	A4
Sedgefield	5	D3
Seghill	5	D1
Selkirk	8	C3
Sellafield	3	E4
Sellafirth	23	F1
Setter	23	E3
Sgiogarstaigh	21	F1
Shap	4	A3
Shawbost (Siabost)	21	E1
Sherburn	5	D2
Shettleston	**25**	**E2**
Shiel Bridge	15	D4
Shieldaig	14	C2
Shilbottle	9	F4
Shildon	4	C3
Shinness Lodge	18	C3
Shiremoor	5	D1
Shotts	8	A2
Siabost (Shawbost)	21	E1
Silloth	3	E2
Silverburn	**25**	**E5**
Siulaisiadar	21	F2
Skaill (East Coast) Ork.	22	C3
Skaill (West Coast) Ork.	22	A3
Skaw	23	F2
Skelmorlie	7	E1
Skelton	5	E3
Skelwick	22	B2
Skerray	18	C1
Skipness	6	C2
Slamannan	8	A1
Sleights	5	F4
Sligachan	14	B3
Smailholm	9	D3
Solas (Sollas)	20	B1
Sollas (Solas)	20	B1
Sorbie	2	B2
Sorisdale	10	B2
Sorn	7	F3
South Bank	5	E3
South Hetton	5	D2
South Kirkton	**24**	**A2**
South Queensferry	8	B1
South Queensferry	**25**	**D4**
South Shields	5	D1
Southdean	9	D4
Southend	6	C4
Spean Bridge	11	F1
Spennymoor	5	D3
Spey Bay	16	C2
Spinningdale	16	A1
Spittal	19	E2
Spittal of Glenshee	12	C2
Springburn	**25**	**E2**
Springholm	3	D1
Springside	7	E3
Stadhlaigearraidh (Stilligarry)	20	A2
Staffin	14	B2
Staindrop	4	C3
Staintondale	5	F4
Stalling Busk	4	B4
Stamfordham	4	C1
Stand	**25**	**F2**
Stane	8	A2
Stanhope	4	B2
Stanley Dur.	4	C2
Stanley P.& K.	12	C3
Stannington	4	C1
Startforth	4	C3
Stenhousemuir	8	A1
Stenness	23	D2
Stenton	9	D1
Steornabhagh (Stornoway)	21	F2
Stepps	**25**	**E2**
Stevenston	7	E2
Stewarton	7	E2
Stichill	9	D3
Stilligarry (Stadhlaigearraidh)	20	A2
Stirling	12	B4
Stobo	8	B3
Stocksfield	4	C2
Stockton-on-Tees	5	D3
Stoer	18	A3
Stokesley	5	E4
Stonefield	**25**	**E3**
Stonehaven	13	F1
Stonehouse	7	G2
Stoneykirk	2	A2
Stoneywood	**24**	**B1**
Stonybreck	23	D4
Stornoway (Steornabhagh)	21	F2
Stow	8	C2
Strachan	13	E1
Strachur	11	E4
Straiton	**25**	**E5**
Straloch	12	C2
Stranraer	2	A2
Strathaven	7	G2
Strathblane	7	F1
Strathdon	16	C4
Strathmiglo	12	C4
Strathpeffer	15	F2
Strathy	19	D1
Strathyre	12	A4
Strichen	17	F2
Stromeferry	14	C3
Stromness	22	A3
Stronachlachar	11	F4
Strone	7	E1
Strontian	11	D2
Stuartfield	17	F3
Sumburgh	23	E4
Sunderland	5	D2
Sunnyside	**24**	**B3**
Swinton	9	D2
Symbister	23	F3
Symington S.Ayr.	7	E3
Symington S.Lan.	8	A3
Syre	18	C2

T

Name	Page	Grid
Tabost (Harbost)	21	F1
Tain	16	A1
Talisker	14	A3
Talladale	15	D2
Tannadice	13	E2
Tannochside	**25**	**F2**
Taobh Tuath (Northton)	21	D3
Tarbert (Jura) Arg. & B.	6	B1
Tarbert (Kintyre) Arg. & B.	6	C1
Tarbert (An Tairbeart) W.Isles	21	E3
Tarbet	11	F4
Tarbolton	7	F3
Tarfside	13	E1
Tarrel	16	B1
Tarves	17	E3
Tavelty	**24**	**A1**
Tayinloan	6	C2
Taynuilt	11	E3
Tayport	13	D3
Tayport	**24**	**B5**
Tayvallich	6	C1
Teangue	14	C4
Tebay	4	A4
Teesside Int Airport	5	D3
Temple Sowerby	4	A3
Teviothead	8	C4
Thainstone House	**24**	**A1**
The Birks	**24**	**A2**
The Neuk	**24**	**A3**
Thornaby-on-Tees	5	D3
Thornhill D. & G.	8	A4
Thornhill Stir.	12	A4
Thornley	5	D2
Thornliebank	**25**	**D3**
Thornton	13	D4
Thorntonhall	**25**	**D3**
Threlkeld	3	F3
Thriepley	**24**	**A4**
Thropton	9	E4
Thrumster	19	F2
Thursby	3	F2
Thurso	19	E1
Thwaite	4	B4
Tibbermore	12	C3
Tighnabruaich	6	D1
Tillicoultry	12	B4
Tillyfourie	17	D4
Timsgearraidh	21	D2
Tingwall	22	B3
Toab	23	E4
Tobermory	10	C2
Toberonochy	11	D4
Todhills	**24**	**B4**
Toft	23	E2
Togston	9	F4
Tolastadh a'Chaolais	21	E2
Tolastadh Úr	21	F1
Toll of Birness	17	F3
Tollcross	**25**	**E2**
Tomatin	16	A3
Tomich	16	A2
Tomintoul	16	C4
Tomnavoulin	16	C3
Tongland	2	C2
Tongue	18	C2
Tore	15	F2
Tormore	6	C3
Torphichen	8	A1
Torphins	17	D4
Torrance E.Dun.	7	F1
Torrance E.Dun.	**25**	**E1**
Torrance S.Lan.	**25**	**E1**
Torridon	15	D2
Torrin	14	B4
Torry	**24**	**C2**
Torthorwald	3	E1
Torver	3	F4
Toscaig	14	C3
Tow Law	4	C2
Town Yetholm	9	E3
Townhead of Greenlaw	4	C2
Tranent	8	C1
Tressait	12	B2
Trimdon	5	D3
Trinity	13	E2
Trochry	12	C3
Troon	7	E3
Troutbeck	3	F4
Troutbeck Bridge	3	F4
Tummel Bridge	12	B2
Tunga	21	F2
Turnberry	7	E4
Turriff	17	E2
Twatt	22	A2
Twechar	7	G1
Twechar	**25**	**E1**
Tweedmouth	9	E2
Tweedsmuir	8	B3
Twynholm	2	C2
Tyndrum	11	F3
Tynemouth	5	D1

U

Name	Page	Grid
Uachdar	20	B2
Uddingston	7	G2
Uddingston	**25**	**E2**
Uddington	8	A3
Uig	14	B2
Ulbster	19	F2
Ulgham	9	F4
Ullapool	15	D1
Ulpha	3	E4
Ulsta	23	E2
Unapool	18	B2
Upper Burnhaugh	**24**	**B3**
Upper Knockando	16	C3
Upper Muirskie	**24**	**B3**
Upper Victoria	**24**	**C4**
Urafirth	23	E2
Ushaw Moor	4	C2
Uyeasound	23	F1

V

Name	Page	Grid
Valsgarth	23	F1
Veensgarth	23	E3
Vidlin	23	F2
Viewpark	**25**	**F2**
Voe	23	E2

W

Name	Page	Grid
Walls	23	E3
Wallsend	5	D1
Wallyford	**25**	**F4**
Warcop	4	A3
Wark	4	B1
Warkworth	9	F4
Warwick Bridge	3	F2
Wasbister	22	B2
Washington	5	D2
Watchgate	4	A4
Waterbeck	3	F1
Waterfoot	**25**	**D3**
Waterside	**25**	**E1**
Watten	19	F2
Wattston	**25**	**F2**
Weem	12	B2
Wellbank	**24**	**B4**
Wemyss Bay	7	E1
Wensley	4	C3
West Auckland	4	C3
West Calder	8	A2
West Kilbride	7	E2
West Linton	8	B2
West Park	**24**	**A3**
West Tarbert	6	C1
West Yell	23	E2
Wester Fintray	**24**	**B1**
Wester Ord	**24**	**B2**
Westerdale	19	E2
Westgate	4	B2
Westhill	17	E4
Westhill	**24**	**B2**
Westness	22	B2
Westnewton	3	E2
Westruther	9	D2
Westside	**24**	**B3**
Wetheral	4	C1
Whalton	4	C1
Whauphill	2	B2
Wheatley Hill	5	D2
Whickham	4	C2
Whifflet	**25**	**F2**
Whitburn	8	A2
Whitby	5	F3
Whitecairns	**24**	**C1**
Whitecraig	8	C1
Whitecraig	**25**	**F4**
Whitehall	22	C2
Whitehaven	3	D3
Whitehills	17	E2
Whiterashes	17	E4
Whithorn	2	B2
Whiting Bay	6	D3
Whitley Bay	5	D1
Whittingham	9	E4
Wick	19	F2
Wigton	3	F2
Wigtown	2	B2
Wilkieston	**25**	**D5**
Willington	4	C3
Winchburgh	8	B1
Windermere	3	F4
Windygates	13	D4
Wingate	5	D2
Winston	4	C3
Winton	4	B3
Wishaw	8	A2
Witton Gilbert	4	C2
Wolsingham	4	C2
Woodhaven	**24**	**B5**
Woodland	4	C3
Woodside	**24**	**C2**
Wooler	9	E3
Workington	3	E3
Wormit	13	D3
Wormit	**24**	**A5**
Wrelton	5	F4

Y

Name	Page	Grid
Yarm	5	D3
Yarrow	8	C3
Yetts o' Muckhart	12	C4
Yoker	**25**	**D2**

Abbreviations used in town plan indexes

All	Alley
App	Approach
Arc	Arcade
Av	Avenue
Bk	Bank
Bldgs	Buildings
Boul	Boulevard
Bri	Bridge
Cen	Central/Centre
Cft	Croft
Ch	Church
Circ	Circus
Clo	Close
Coll	College
Cor	Corner
Cotts	Cottages
Cres	Crescent
Ct	Court
Dr	Drive
E	East
Esp	Esplanade
Est	Estate
Ex	Exchange
Fm	Farm
Gdn	Garden
Gdns	Gardens
Gra	Grange
Grn	Green
Gro	Grove
Hts	Heights
Ho	House
Hos	Hospital
Ind	Industrial
Junct	Junction
La	Lane
Ln	Loan
Mans	Mansion
Mkt	Market
Ms	Mews
Mt	Mount
N	North
Par	Parade
Pk	Park
Pl	Place
Quad	Quadrant
Rd	Road
Ri	Rise
S	South
Sch	School
Sq	Square
St	Street
St.	Saint
Sta	Station
Ter	Terrace
Twr	Tower
Vills	Villas
Vw	View
W	West
Wd	Wood
Wds	Woods
Wf	Wharf
Wk	Walk
Wks	Works
Yd	Yard

KEY TO MAP SYMBOLS

Symbol	Description
M74	Motorway
A82	Primary road dual / single
A70	'A' Road dual / single
B793	'B' Road dual / single
	Other road dual / single
Toll →	One-way street / Toll
	Restricted access / Pedestrian street
	Minor road / Track
FB	Footpath / Cycle path / Footbridge
	Railway line / station
	Railway tunnel / Level crossing
	Bus / Coach station
P	Car Park
	Leisure / Tourism
	Shopping / Retail
	Administration / Law
	Education
	Hospital
	Industry / Commerce
	Notable building
	Health centre
Pol PO Lib	Police station / Post Office / Library
+ ☾ ✡	Church / Mosque / Synagogue
	Cinema / Theatre
Hilton	Major Hotel
i i	Tourist information centre (all year / seasonal)
	Fire station / Ambulance station / Community centre

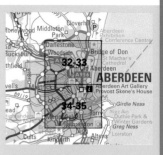

Maps 32-35   Index 36-37
Scale 4 inches to 1 mile

ABERDEEN

Maps 38-39   Index 40-41
Scale 4.6 inches to 1 mile

DUNDEE

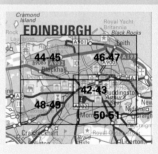

Maps 42-51   Index 52-57
Scale 4 inches to 1 mile
City centre map 5.7 inches to 1 mile

EDINBURGH

Maps 58-65   Index 66-72
Scale 4 inches to 1 mile

GLASGOW

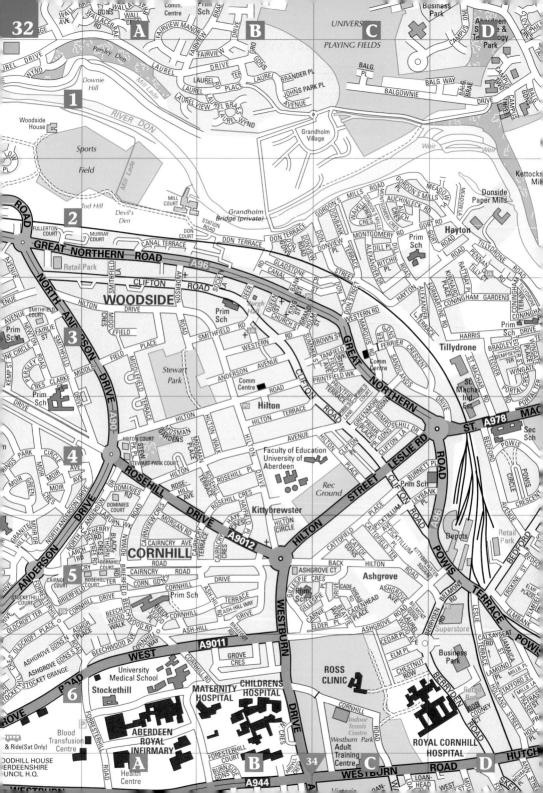

Scotsdown Medical Centre

Prim Sch

Sec Sch

B997

Comm Cen

Comm Cen

NORTH DONSIDE ROAD

NORTH DO

ELLON ROAD

MINS CLOSE

Barracks

ALMA ROAD

CORUNNA ROAD

Royal Aberdeen Golf Club Clubhouse

Danestone Terrace

Danestone

Bellfield Rd

Sec Sch

Simpson

Hutcheon

Pleasant

Mount

Balgownie Road

Balgownie Crescent

Donmouth Ct

Donm Cres

Donm Gdns

Donmouth Road

RIVER DON

Hillhead Halls of Residence

Brig o' Balgownie

Cottown of Balgownie

KEITH PARK

SEATON PARK

ESPLANADE

Bridge Of Don

Weir

Wallace Tower

Tillydrone Road

Tillydrone Ave

O.T.C. Building

Computer Centre

Dunbar Hall

St Machar's Cathedral

Mitchell's Hospital

Cruickshank Botanic Gardens

Lord Hay's Grove

Inverdon Court

St Ninians

Lord Hay's Court

St Ninians Court

Balgownie Court

Livingstone Court

Prim Sch

KINGS LINKS

GOLF COURSE

University

School of Agriculture

King's College

Crombie-Johnston Hall

Meston Walk

Hermitage Ave

Elphinstone Rd

High St

Dunbar St

College Bounds

UNIVERSITY ROAD

KING STREET

SEATON PLACE EAST

HARROW RD

CHEYNE RD

Prim Sch

Chanonry

Don

Dunbar

St Machar

Seaton Place

Seaton St

SEATON AVE

SEAT GDNS

SEATON

SEATON DRIVE

Beachview Court

Aulton Court

Northsea Court

Donview House

Seaton House

Seaview House

Bayview Court

Crescent

SCHOOL ROAD

SCHOOL DRIVE

SCHOOL AVE

REGENT WALK

SCHOOL WALK

Linksfield Court

Promenade Court

Regent Court

School for the Deaf

Sec Sch and Baths

Chris Anderson Stadium

Linksfield Gdns

Links View

Linksfield Road

Ardaproch Place

Links Road

ESPLANADE

GOLF ROAD

Sunnyside

Orchard Walk

Orchard Place

Spital Walk

Orchard Street

Sunnybank

Prim Sch

Sunnyside Terrace

Sunnybank Ave

Embankment Pl

Firhill Road

St Peter's Cem

St Peter's

Froghall View

Froghall Terrace

Pittodrie Place

Pittodrie Lane

Pittodrie

Merkland Road

Merkland La

Merkland Road East

Merkland La

Aberdeen A.F.C. (Pittodrie Park)

Clubhouse

BROAD HILL

Lynx Ice Arena

Beach Leisure Centre

Beach Ballroom

Errol Pl

Errol St

Peter La

St Peter St

Advocates

Jute Street

Frog St

Kings Crescent

Mounthooly Way

Nelson St

Nelson La

Fire Sta

Seaforth Road

Bodie

Prim Sch

Urquhart Road

Urquhart St

Urquhart La

Urquhart Ter

Trinity Cemetery

CITY HOSPITAL

Links Road

Bowling Green

Tennis Courts

PLACE

CAUSEWAYEND

WEST N

STREET

KING STREET

A956

Canal Road

Canal St

Catherine

Willowdale

Nelson St

Roslin St

Roslin

Duke St

Jasmine Way

Jasmine Ter

Park Road

Prim Sch

Hutcheon Court

Greig Court

Gerrard Street

Spring Garden

Bradford Works

Kingsland Place

Catherine St

Gordon

Lewis

E F G H

1 2 3 4 5 6

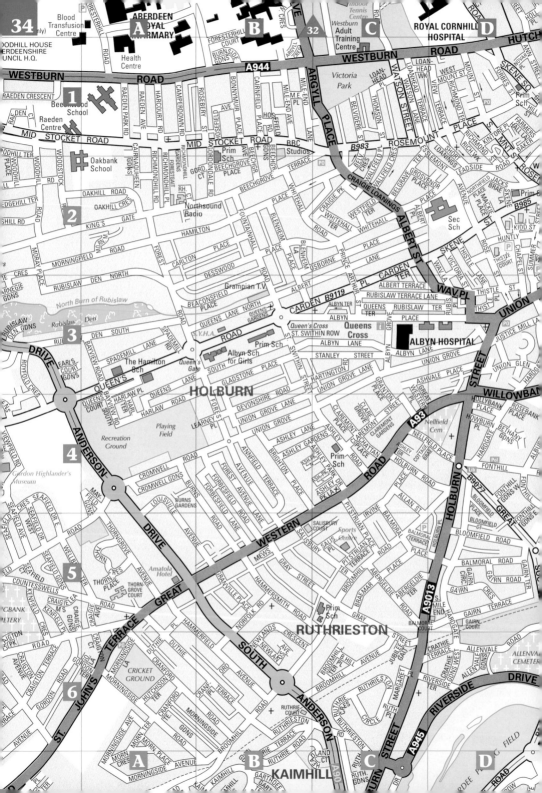

A

Abbey La 35 H4
Abbey Pl 35 H4
Abbey Rd 35 H4
Abbey Sq 35 H4
Abbotsford La 35 E4
Abergeldie Rd 34 C5
Abergeldie Ter 34 C5
Academy St 35 E3
Advocates Rd 33 F6
Albert La 34 B3
Albert Pl 34 C2
Albert Quay 35 G3
Albert St 34 C2
Albert Ter 34 C3
Albury Pl 35 E4
Albury Rd 34 D4
Albyn Gro 34 C3
Albyn La 34 C3
Albyn Pl 34 C3
Albyn Ter 34 C3
Alexander Dr 32 C2
Alexander Ter 32 C3
Allan St 34 C4
Allenvale Gdns 34 D6
Allenvale Rd 34 D6
Anderson Av 32 B3
Anderson Rd 32 A2
Annfield Ter 34 B4
Ann St 34 D1
Ardarroch Pl 33 G5
Ardarroch Rd 33 F5
Argyll Cres 34 B1
Argyll Pl 34 B1
Ashgrove Av 32 C5
Ashgrove Ct 32 B5
Ashgrove Rd 32 C5
Ash-hill Dr 32 A5
Ash-hill Rd 32 B5
Ash-hill Way 32 B5
Ashley Gdns 34 B4
Ashley Gro 34 C4
Ashley La 34 B4
Ashley Pk Dr 34 B4
Ashley Pk La 34 C4
Ashley Pk N 34 B4
Ashley Pk S 34 C4
Ashley Rd 34 C4
Ashvale Pl 34 C3
Auchinleck Cres 32 C2
Auchinleck Rd 32 C2
Aulton Ct 33 G3

B

Back Hilton Rd 32 C5
Back Wynd 35 E2
Baker St 34 D1
Balgownie Brae 32 D1
Balgownie Ct 33 F3
Balgownie Cres 33 F1
Balgownie Dr 32 C1
Balgownie Gdns 32 D1
Balgownie Pl 32 C1
Balgownie Rd 33 F1
Balgownie Way 32 C1
Balmoral Ct 34 C5
Balmoral Pl 34 C5
Balmoral Rd 34 D5
Balmoral Ter 34 C5
Balnagask Rd 35 H5
Baltic Pl 35 H2
Baltic St 35 G2
Bank St 35 E4
Bank St 32 B3
(Woodside)
Battock Pl 35 G5
Baxter St 35 H4
Bayview Ct 33 G4
Bayview Rd 34 A3
Bayview Rd S 34 A4
Beach Boul 35 G1
Beachview Ct 34 C5
Beaconsfield Pl 34 A3
Beattie Av 32 C5
Bedford Av 32 D4
Bedford Pl 32 D5
Bedford Rd 32 D5
Beechgrove Av 34 B2
Beechgrove Gdns 34 B1
Beechgrove Pl 34 B2

Beechgrove Ter 34 B2
Beechwood Av 32 A6
Beechwood Pl 32 A5
Beechwood Rd 32 A5
Beechwood Wk 32 A5
Belgrave Ter 34 C2
Belmont Gdns 32 C5
Belmont Rd 32 D5
Belmont St 35 E2
Belvidere Cres 34 C2
Belvidere St 34 C1
Berryden Rd 32 D6
Berry St 35 F1
Bethany Gdns 34 D4
Blackfriars St 35 E1
Blacks La 35 G3
Blackthorn Cres 32 A5
Blaikies Quay 35 G2
Blenheim La 34 B2
Blenheim Pl 34 B2
Bloomfield Ct 34 D5
Bloomfield Pl 34 D4
Bloomfield Rd 34 D5
Bob Cooney Ct 32 D6
Boddie Pl 33 F6
Bon Accord Cres 35 E3
Bon Accord St 35 E3
Bonnymuir Pl 34 B1
Bradley Ter 32 D3
Braefoot Rd 32 B5
Braemar Pl 34 C5
Brander Pl 32 B1
Bridge of Don 33 G2
Bridge St 35 E2
Brierfield Rd 32 A5
Brighton Pl 34 B4
Bright St 35 E5
Brig o' Balgownie 33 F1
Brimmond Pl 35 G5
Broomhill Av 34 C6
Broomhill Pl 34 C6
Broomhill Rd 34 C5
Broomhill Ter 34 C6
Brown St 32 C3
Brunswick Pl 35 E5
Burnbank Pl 35 H5
Burnbank Ter 35 H5
Burnett Pl 32 C4
Burns Gdns 34 A4
Burnside Gdns 34 B1
Burns Rd 34 A4

C

Cadenhead Pl 32 C5
Cadenhead Rd 32 C5
Cairnaquheen 34 A1
Gdns
Cairncry Av 32 A5
Cairncry Cres 32 B5
Cairncry Rd 32 A5
Cairncry Ter 32 A5
Cairnfield Pl 34 B1
Cairnfold Rd 33 E1
Cairnview Cres 32 A5
Caledonian Pl 35 E4
Calsayseat Rd 32 D6
Camperdown Rd 34 A1
Campus One 32 D1
Campus Three 32 D1
Campus Two 32 D1
Canal Pl 33 E6
Canal Rd 33 E6
Canal St 33 E6
Canal St 32 B2
(Woodside)
Canal Ter 32 A2
Carden Pl 34 B3
Carden Ter 34 C3
Carlton Pl 34 A2
Carnie Dr 32 B5
Castle Ter 35 G2
Catherine St 35 E1
Cattofield Gdns 32 C5
Cattofield Pl 32 C5
Cattofield Ter 32 C5
Causewayend 33 E6
Cedar Pl 32 D5
Chanonry 33 E3
Chapel St 34 D2
Charles St 33 E6
Charlotte Gdns 35 E1

Charlotte St 35 E1
Chattan Pl 34 C4
Cherry Rd 32 A5
Chestnut Row 32 C6
Cheyne Rd 33 F3
Church St 35 G2
Church St 32 B3
(Woodside)
Claremont Gdns 34 C4
Claremont Gro 34 C4
Claremont Pl 34 C4
Claremont St 34 C4
Clarence St 35 G2
Clarks La 33 F3
Clifton La 32 C4
Clifton Pl 32 C4
Clifton Rd 32 A3
Clyde St 35 G3
College Bounds 33 E4
College St 35 E3
Colville Pl 33 F6
Commerce St 35 G2
Commercial Quay 35 G3
Coningham Gdns 32 D3
Coningham Rd 32 D3
Coningham Ter 32 D3
Constitution St 35 G1
Cornhill Ct 32 A5
Cornhill Dr 32 A5
Cornhill Gdns 32 A5
Cornhill Rd 32 A6
Cornhill Ter 32 A5
Cornhill Way 32 A6
Corsehill Gdns 32 D1
Corunna Rd 33 G1
Cottage Brae 34 C4
Cotton St 35 G1
Cottown of 33 F1
Balgownie
Coull Gdns 33 E1
Craigelea Av 34 A5
Craigie Loanings 34 C2
Craigie Pk 34 C2
Craigie St 35 E1
Craigton Ct 34 A6
Cranford Pl 34 B6
Cranford Rd 34 A6
Cranford Ter 34 B6
Crathie Gdns W 34 D6
Crathie Ter 34 C6
Crimon Pl 35 E2
Crombie Pl 35 G4
Crombie Rd 35 G4
Cromwell Gdns 34 A4
Cromwell Rd 34 A4
Crooked La 35 E1
Crown St 35 E3
Crown Ter 35 E3

D

Danestone Pl 33 F1
Danestone Ter 33 F1
Davan Pk 33 E1
Deemount Av 35 E5
Deemount Gdns 35 E5
Deemount Rd 35 E5
Deemount Ter 35 E5
Dee Pl 35 E3
Deer Rd 32 B3
Dee St 35 E3
Dempsey Ter 32 D3
Denburn Rd 35 E1
Denmore Gdns 33 E1
Desswood Pl 34 B3
Devanha Cres 35 E4
Devanha Gdns 35 E4
Devanha Gdns E 35 E4
Devanha Gdns S 35 E5
Devanha Gdns W 35 E4
Devanha Ter 35 E4
Devonshire Rd 34 B4
Diamond St 35 E2
Dill Pl 32 C2
Dill Rd 32 C2
Dominies Ct 32 A4
Dominies Rd 32 A4
Donbank Ter 32 C2
Don Ct 32 A2
Don Gdns 32 B2
Donmouth Ct 33 G1
Donmouth Cres 33 G1

Donmouth Gdns 33 G1
Donmouth Rd 33 G1
Donmouth Ter 33 G1
Don Pl 32 C3
Don St 33 E3
(Old Aberdeen)
Don St 32 C3
(Woodside)
Don Ter 32 B2
Donview Ho 33 G3
Donview Pl 32 C2
Donview Rd 32 B2
Downies Brae 35 G5
Downies Pl 35 H5
Duff St 35 G1
Dunbar St 33 E4
Duthie Pl 34 A6
Duthie Ter 34 A6

E

East N St 35 F1
East Tullos Ind Est 35 H6
Elder Pl 32 B5
Elmbank Rd 33 E6
Elmbank Ter 32 D5
Elmfield Av 32 D5
Elmfield Pl 32 D5
Elmfield Ter 32 D5
Elm Pl 32 C6
Elphinstone Rd 33 E4
Errol Pl 33 F6
Errol St 33 F6
Erskine St 32 D5
Esplanade 35 H2
Esslemont Av 34 C1
Exchange St 35 F2

F

Fairview Brae 32 A1
Fairview Dr 32 B1
Farmers Hall La 34 D1
Farquhar Av 35 H5
Farquhar Brae 35 H5
Farquhar Rd 35 H5
Fernie Brae 35 G6
Ferrier Cres 32 C3
Ferrier Gdns 32 C3
Ferryhill Gdns 35 E4
Ferryhill La 35 E4
Ferryhill Pl 35 E4
Ferryhill Rd 35 E4
Ferryhill Ter 35 E4
Ferry Pl 35 H3
Firhill Rd 33 E5
Fish St 35 F2
Fonthill Gdns E 34 D5
Fonthill Gdns W 34 D4
Fonthill Rd 34 D4
Fonthill Ter 34 D4
Forbesfield La 34 B4
Forbesfield Rd 34 B4
Forbes St 34 D1
Forest Av 34 B4
Forest Av La 34 B4
Foresterhill Ct 34 B1
Forestgait 34 A2
Forest Rd 34 A2
Formartine Rd 32 C3
Forresterhill Rd 34 A2
Fountainhall Rd 34 B2
Fowlershill Gdns 33 E1
Fraser Ct 33 E6
Fraserfield Gdns 33 E1
Fraser Pl 32 D6
Fraser Rd 32 D6
Fraser St 32 D6
Frederick St 35 F1
Froghall Av 33 E6
Froghall Gdns 33 E6
Froghall Pl 33 E6
Froghall Rd 33 E6
Froghall Ter 33 E6
Froghall Vw 35 E5

G

Gairn Circle 34 D5
Gairn Ct 34 D5
Gairn Cres 34 D5
Gairn Rd 34 D5
Gairn Ter 34 D5
Gallowgate 35 F1

Garvock Wynd 35 H2
George St 33 E6
Gerrard St 35 E1
Gilcomston Steps 34 D1
Gillespie Cres 32 B5
Gillespie Pl 32 B5
Girdleness Rd 35 H5
Girdleness Ter 35 G6
Girdlestone Pl 35 H5
Gladstone Pl 34 B3
Gladstone Pl 32 B2
(Woodside)
Glenbervie Rd 35 G4
Golf Rd 33 G5
Gordondale Ct 34 A2
Gordondale Rd 34 B1
Gordon La 34 A6
Gordon's Mills 32 C2
Cres
Gordon's Mills Pl 32 C2
Gordon's Mills Rd 32 C2
Gordon St 35 E3
Gort Rd 32 C2
Grampian La 35 G4
Grampian Pl 35 F5
Grampian Rd 35 G5
Grandholm Br 32 B2
(Private)
Grandholm St 32 B3
Granton Pl 34 C3
Granville Pl 34 B5
Gray St 34 B5
Gray St Ms 34 B5
Great Northern Rd 32 C3
Great Southern Rd 34 D5
Great Western Pl 34 C4
Great Western Rd 34 A5
Greenmore Gdns 32 C4
Greenwell Pl 35 H6
Greenwell Rd 35 H6
Gregness Gdns 35 H6
Greig Ct 35 E1
Grosvenor Pl 34 C2
Grove Cres 32 B6
Guild St 35 F3

H

Hamilton Pl 34 A2
Hammerfield Av 34 A5
Hammersmith Rd 34 B5
Hanover St 35 G1
Harcourt Rd 34 A1
Hardgate 34 D4
Harlaw Pl 34 A4
Harlaw Rd 34 A4
Harlaw Ter 34 A4
Harriet St 35 E2
Harris Dr 32 D3
Harrow Rd 33 F3
Hartington Rd 34 B3
Hayfield Cres 32 B5
Hayfield Pl 32 B4
Hayton Rd 32 C3
Hermitage Av 33 E4
Highgate Gdns 35 F5
High St 33 E4
Hill St 34 D1
Hill Vw Gdns 35 G6
Hillview Rd 35 G6
Hilton Av 32 A4
Hilton Circle 32 B5
Hilton Ct 32 A4
Hilton Dr 32 B4
Hilton Pl 32 C4
Hilton Rd 32 A4
Hilton St 32 B5
Hilton Ter 32 B4
Hilton Wk 32 B4
Holburn Pl 34 D5
Holburn Rd 34 C4
Holburn St 34 D5
Holland Pl 32 D6
Holland St 32 D6
Hollybank Pl 34 D4
Hosefield Av 34 B1
Hosefield Rd 34 B1
Howburn Pl 34 D4
Hunter Pl 33 F6
Huntly St 34 D2
Hutcheon Ct 33 E6
Hutcheon Gdns 33 F1

Hutcheon St 34 D1	Marischal St 35 F2	Polmuir Rd 35 E4	St. Machar Dr 32 D4	Thistle La 34 D2
Hutchison Ter 34 A6	Market St 35 F2	Polwarth Rd 35 F5	St. Machar Ind Est 32 D3	Thistle Pl 34 D3
	Marquis Rd 32 C3	Portal Cres 32 D3	St. Machar Pl 33 F3	Thistle St 34 D3
I	Matthews Quay 35 H3	Portal Ter 32 D4	St. Machar Rd 32 D3	Thomas Glover Pl 33 E1
Inverdon Ct 33 F2	Mayfield Gdns 34 A4	Portland St 35 E3	St. Nicholas Cen 35 F2	Thomson St 34 C1
Irvine Pl 34 C5	Meadow La 32 D2	Powis Circle 32 D4	St. Ninians Ct 33 F3	Thorngrove Av 34 A5
	Meadow Pl 32 C2	Powis Cres 32 D4	St. Ninians Pl 33 F2	Thorngrove Ct 34 A5
J	Mearns Quay 35 H3	Powis La 33 E6	St. Peter La 33 F6	Thorngrove Cres 34 A5
Jacks Brae 34 D2	Mearns St 35 G2	Powis Pl 32 D6	St. Peter's Gate 33 F6	Thorngrove Pl 34 A5
Jamaica St 32 D6	Menzies Rd 35 G4	Powis Ter 32 D5	St. Peter's Pl 33 F6	Tillydrone Av 33 E3
James St 35 G2	Merkland La 33 G5	Poynernook Rd 35 F3	St. Peter St 33 F6	Tillydrone Ct 32 D2
Jamiesons Quay 35 F3	Merkland Pl 33 F5	Primrosehill Dr 32 C4	St. Swithin Row 34 B3	Tillydrone Rd 33 E3
Jasmine Pl 35 F1	Merkland Rd 33 F5	Primrosehill Gdns 32 C4	St. Swithin St 34 C3	Tillydrone Ter 32 D3
Jasmine Ter 35 F1	Merkland Rd E 33 F5	Primrosehill Pl 32 C4	Salisbury Ct 34 C5	Trinity Quay 35 F2
Jasmine Way 35 F1	Meston Wk 33 E4	Prince Arthur St 34 C2	Salisbury Pl 34 C5	Tullos Circle 35 G5
Johns Pk Pl 32 B1	Midchingle Rd 35 G3	Princes St 35 F1	Salisbury Ter 34 B5	Tullos Cres 35 H5
John St 35 E1	Middlefield Cres 34 A3	Printfield Ter 32 C3	Sandilands Dr 32 C3	Tullos Pl 35 H5
Jopps La 35 E1	Middlefield Ter 32 A3	Printfield Wk 32 C3	School Av 33 F4	
Jubilee Gait 34 C6	Mile-End Av 34 B1	Promenade Ct 33 G4	School Dr 33 F4	**U**
Justice Mill La 34 D3	Mile-End La 34 B1	Prospect Ct 35 F4	Schoolhill 35 E2	Union Glen 34 D3
Jute St 33 E6	Mile-End Pl 34 B1	Prospect Ter 35 F4	School Rd 33 F4	Union Gro 34 C3
	Millbank La 32 D6		School Ter 33 F4	Union Gro La 34 C4
K	Millbank Pl 32 D6	**Q**	School Wk 33 G4	Union Row 34 D3
Kerloch Gdns 35 F5	Millburn St 35 E4	Queen 35 F4	Scotstown Gdns 33 F1	Union St 34 D3
Kerloch Pl 35 F5	Mill Ct 32 A2	Elizabeth II Br	Seaforth Rd 33 F6	Union Ter 35 E2
Kettocks Mill Rd 33 E2	Miller St 35 G2	Queens Ct 34 A4	Seamount Rd 35 F1	Union Wynd 34 D2
Kidd St 34 D2	Montgomery Cres 32 C2	Queen's Cross 34 B3	Seaton Av 33 F3	University Rd 33 E4
King George VI Br 35 E6	Montgomery Rd 32 C2	Queens Gdns 34 B3	Seaton Cres 33 G3	Upperkirkgate 35 F2
Kings Cres 33 F6	Morgan Rd 32 A5	Queen's Gate 34 A3	Seaton Dr 33 F3	Urquhart La 33 F6
King's Gate 34 A2	Morningfield Ms 34 A2	Queens La N 34 B3	Seaton Gdns 33 F3	Urquhart Pl 33 G6
Kingsland Pl 35 E1	Morningside Gdns 34 A6	Queens La S 34 A3	Seaton Ho 33 G3	Urquhart Rd 33 F6
King St 33 F5	Morningside La 34 A6	Queens Links 35 H1	Seaton Pl 33 F3	Urquhart St 33 G6
King St (Woodside) 32 B3	Morningside Pl 34 A6	Leisure Pk	Seaton Pl E 33 F3	Urquhart Ter 33 G6
Kinnaird Pl 32 D2	Morningside Rd 34 A6	Queens Ter 34 C3	Seaton Rd 33 F3	
Kinord Circle 33 E1	Morningside Ter 34 A6	Queen St 35 F2	Seaton Wk 33 F3	**V**
Kintore Pl 34 D1	Morven Pl 35 G5	Queen St 32 B3	Seaview Ho 33 G4	Victoria Br 35 G3
Kirkhill Pl 35 H6	Mosman Gdns 32 A4	(Woodside)	Seaview Rd 33 F1	Victoria Rd 35 G4
Kirkhill Rd 35 G6	Mosman Pl 32 A4		Shiprow 35 F2	Victoria St 34 D2
Kittybrewster Sq 32 C5	Mounthooly 33 F6	**R**	Short Loanings 34 D1	View Ter 34 D1
	Mounthooly Way 33 F6	Raeburn Pl 35 E1	Simpson Rd 33 F1	Virginia St 35 F2
L	Mount Pleasant 33 G1	Raeden Av 34 A1	Sinclair Pl 35 H4	
Laburnum Wk 32 A5	Mount St 34 D1	Raeden Pk Rd 34 A1	Sinclair Rd 35 G4	**W**
Ladywell Pl 35 H5	Murray Ct 32 A2	Raik Rd 35 F3	Skene La 34 D2	Wales St 35 G1
Lamond Pl 32 D6	Murray Ter 35 E5	Rattray Pl 32 D2	Skene Sq 34 D1	Walker La 35 G4
Langstane Pl 35 E3		Regent Ct 33 G4	Skene St 34 D2	Walker Pl 35 G4
Laurel Av 32 B1	**N**	Regent Quay 35 G2	Skene Ter 35 E2	Walker Rd 35 F5
Laurel Braes 32 B1	Nellfield Pl 34 C4	Regent Rd 35 G3	Smithfield La 34 A3	Wallfield Cres 34 C2
Laurel Dr 32 A1	Nelson Ct 33 F6	Regent Wk 33 F4	Smithfield Rd 32 A3	Wallfield Pl 34 C2
Laurel Gdns 32 B1	Nelson La 33 F6	Richmondhill Ct 34 A2	Society La 32 B3	Wapping St 35 E2
Laurel Gro 32 B1	Nelson St 33 F6	Richmondhill Gdns 34 A1	South Anderson Dr 34 B6	Waterloo Quay 35 G2
Laurel Pl 32 A1	Newlands Av 34 B6	Richmondhill Pl 34 A1	South Coll St 35 F3	Watson La 34 C1
Laurel Rd 32 A1	Newlands Cres 34 B6	Richmondhill Rd 34 A1	South Crown St 35 E4	Watson St 34 C1
Laurel Ter 32 B1	Norfolk Rd 34 B5	Richmond St 34 D1	South Esplanade E 35 G4	Wavell Cres 32 C2
Laurel Vw 32 A1	North Esplanade E 35 G3	Richmond Ter 34 D1	South Esplanade W 35 F4	Waverley La 34 C2
Laurelwood Av 32 C5	North Esplanade W 35 F4	Richmond Wk 34 D1	South Grampian 35 G5	Waverley Pl 34 D3
Laurel Wynd 32 B1	Northfield Pl 34 D2	Ritchie Pl 32 C2	Circle	Wellington Brae 35 F4
Leadside Rd 34 D2	North Grampian 32 G5	Riverside Dr 34 D6	South Mile End 34 D5	Wellington Br 35 F5
Learney Pl 34 A4	Circle	Riverside Ter 34 C6	South Mt St 34 D1	Wellington Pl 35 E3
Lemon St 35 G1	Northsea Ct 33 G3	Rockall Pl 35 H5	Spademill La 34 A3	Wellington Rd 35 F5
Leslie Pl 32 C4	Novar Pl 34 D1	Rockall Rd 35 H5	Spademill Rd 34 A3	Wellington St 35 H2
Leslie Ter 32 D5		Rodger's Wk 35 E1	Spa St 35 E1	Westburn Cres 32 B6
Lilybank Pl 32 C4	**O**	Rosebank Pl 34 D4	Spital 33 F5	Westburn Dr 32 B5
Lime St 35 H2	Oakhill Cres 34 A2	Rosebank Ter 35 E4	Spital Wk 33 E5	Westburn Pk 32 C6
Linksfield Ct 33 G4	Oakhill Rd 34 A2	Rosebery St 34 B1	Springbank St 35 E3	Westburn Rd 34 C1
Linksfield Gdns 33 F5	Old Ch Rd 35 G6	Rosehill Av 32 A4	Springbank Ter 35 E3	Western Rd 32 C3
Linksfield Pl 33 F5	Old Ford Rd 35 F4	Rosehill Ct 32 A5	Spring Gdn 35 E1	Westfield Rd 34 C2
Linksfield Rd 33 F5	Orchard Pl 33 E5	Rosehill Cres 32 B4	Stafford St 32 D6	Westfield Ter 34 C2
Links Pl 35 H2	Orchard Rd 33 E5	Rosehill Dr 32 A4	Stanley St 34 C3	West Mt St 34 D1
Links Rd 35 H1	Orchard St 33 E5	Rosehill Pl 32 B4	Station Rd 32 B2	West N St 35 F1
Links Rd 33 G3	Orchard Wk 33 E5	Rosehill Ter 32 B4	Stell Rd 35 F3	Whinhill Gdns 35 E5
(Bridge of Don)	Osborne Pl 34 B2	Rosemount Pl 34 C1	Stewart Pk Ct 32 A4	Whinhill Gate 35 E4
Links St 35 H2	Oscar Pl 35 G5	Rosemount Viaduct 34 D2	Stewart Pk Pl 32 A4	Whinhill Rd 34 D5
Links Vw 33 G5	Oscar Rd 35 G5	Rose St 34 D2	Summerfield Ter 35 F1	Whitehall Pl 34 B2
Livingstone Ct 33 F3		Roslin Pl 35 G1	Summer St 34 D2	Whitehall Rd 34 B2
Loanhead Pl 34 C1	**P**	Roslin St 33 G6	Summer St 32 B3	Whitehall Ter 34 C2
Loanhead Ter 34 C1	Palmerston Pl 35 F4	Roslin Ter 33 F6	(Woodside)	Willowbank Rd 34 D4
Loanhead Wk 34 C1	Palmerston Rd 35 F4	Rowan Rd 32 A5	Sunnybank Pl 33 E5	Willowdale Pl 35 F1
Loch St 35 E1	Park Rd 33 G6	Rubislaw Pl 34 D3	Sunnybank Rd 33 E5	Wingate Pl 32 D3
Loirston Pl 35 H5	Park St 35 G1	Rubislaw Ter 34 C3	Sunnyside Av 33 E5	Wingate Rd 32 D3
Lord Hay's Ct 33 G2	Pennan Rd 32 D2	Rubislaw Ter La 34 C3	Sunnyside Gdns 33 E5	Woolmanhill 35 E2
Lord Hay's Gro 33 F2	Picktillum Av 32 C5	Russell Rd 35 F4	Sunnyside Rd 32 D5	
Louisville Av 34 A4	Picktillum Pl 32 C5	Ruthrie Ct 34 B6	Sunnyside Ter 33 E5	**Y**
	Pirie's Ct 32 A2	Ruthrieston Circle 34 C6	Sycamore Pl 35 E5	York Pl 35 H2
M	Pirie's La 32 C4	Ruthrieston Cres 34 C6		York St 35 H2
Maberly St 35 E1	Pitstruan Pl 34 C4	Ruthrieston Pl 34 C6	**T**	
Mackie Pl 34 D2	Pitstruan Ter 34 C5	Ruthrieston Rd 34 B6	Tanfield Av 32 C3	
Mansfield Pl 35 H5	Pittodrie La 33 F5		Tanfield Wk 32 C3	
Mansfield Rd 35 H4	Pittodrie Pl 33 F5	**S**	Tarbothill Rd 32 D1	
Margaret Pl 34 C6	Pittodrie St 33 F5	St. Andrew St 35 E1	Tedder Rd 32 D3	
Marine Ter 35 E4	Polmuir Av 35 E5	St. Clair St 35 F1	Tedder St 32 D3	
	Polmuir Pl 35 E5	St. Clement St 35 G2	Thistle Ct 34 D2	

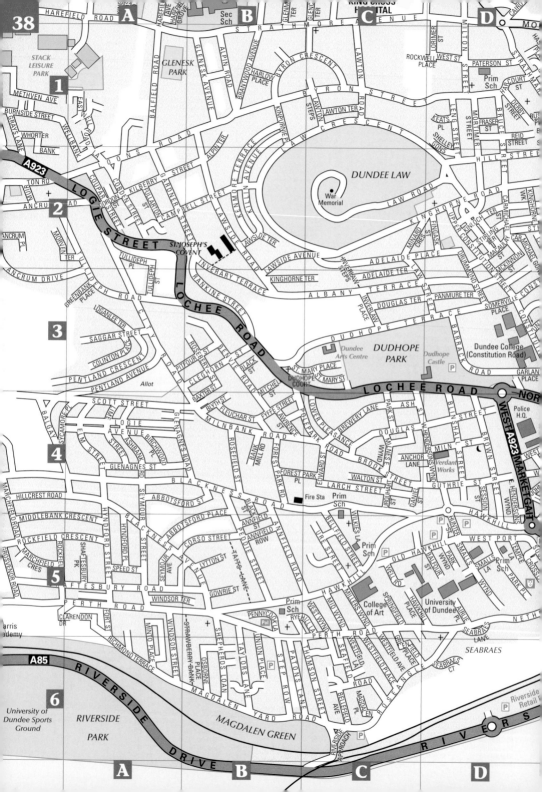

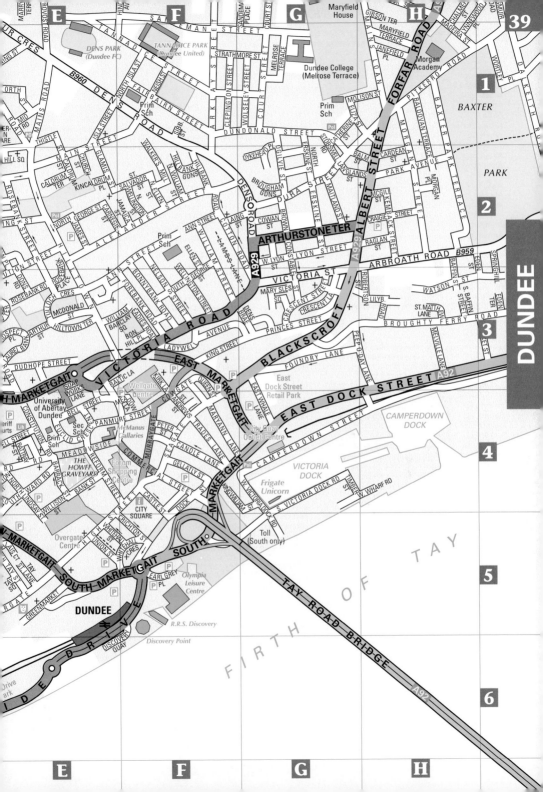

INDEX TO STREETS

This index contains streets that are not named on the map due to insufficient space. For each of these cases the nearest street that does appear on the map is shown in *italics*.

A

Abbotsford Pl 38 A5
Abbotsford St 38 A4
Adelaide Pl 38 C2
Adelaide Ter 38 C3
Airlie Pl 38 D5
Albany Ter 38 C3
Albert Sq 39 F4
  Commercial St
Albert St 39 H2
Alexander St 39 E2
Alpin Rd 38 B1
Alpin Ter 38 B2
Alva Sq 39 E2
Anchor La 38 C4
Annfield Rd 38 B5
Annfield Row 38 B5
Annfield St 38 B5
Ann St 39 E3
Arbroath Rd 39 H2
Arklay St 39 F1
Arthurstone Ter 39 G2
Arthur St 39 E3
Artillery La 38 D5
Ashbank Rd 38 A4
Ash La 38 C4
  Ash St
Ash St 38 C4

B

Baffin St 39 H2
Baffin Ter 39 H2
  Baffin St
Baldovan Ter 39 H1
Balfield Rd 38 A1
Balfour St 38 D5
Balgayview 38 A2
  Gdns
Balmore St 39 G2
Baltic Gdns 38 B6
  Patons La
Baltic La 39 E3
Bank Mill Rd 38 B4
Bank St 39 E4
Barrack Rd 38 D3
Barrack St 39 E4
Baxter Pk Ter 39 H1
Baxter St 38 B4
Bellefield Av 38 C6
Bellfield St 38 C5
Bell St 39 E4
Benvie Rd 38 B3
Birchwood Pl 38 A4
Blackness Av 38 A5
Blackness Rd 38 A4
Blackness St 38 B4
Blackness Ter 38 A5
Blackscroft 39 G3
Black St 38 B3
Blaikies Ms 39 E2
  Alexander St
Blinshall St 38 D4
Blyth Pl 38 B4
Blyth St 38 B4
Bonnethill Ct 39 E3
  Hilltown Ter
Bonnet Hill Pl 39 F3
Bonnybank Rd 39 F3
Brantwood Av 38 B1

Brantwood Pl 38 B1
  Brantwood Av
Brewery La 38 C4
Brook St 38 C4
Brougham 39 G2
  Gdns
Broughty 39 H3
  Ferry Rd
Brown 39 G2
  Constable St
Brown St 38 D4
Bruce St 38 D1
Buchanan St 39 G2
Bucklemaker 38 D1
  Ct
  Harcourt St
Burgess St 38 D1
Butterburn Ct 38 D1
  Strathmartine Rd
Butterburn Sq 38 D1
Byron Cres 38 B1
Byron St 38 B1

C

Caldrum St 39 E2
Caldrum Ter 39 E2
Callender 39 G3
  Gdns
Campbell St 38 A2
Camperdown 39 G4
  St
Candle La 39 F4
Canning Pl 38 D1
Canning St 38 D1
Cardean St 39 H2
Carmichael Ct 38 D2
Carmichael 38 D2
  Gdns
Carmichael St 38 D2
Carnegie Sq 39 E2
  Ann St
Carnegie St 39 E2
Carnegie Twr 39 F2
  Alexander St
Castle St 39 F4
Catherine St 39 G1
Chapel St 39 E4
  Meadowside
Church St 39 E2
City Quay 39 G4
  Outlet Cen
City Rd 38 A3
City Sq 39 F4
Clarendon Dr 38 A5
Clarendon Ter 38 A5
Cleghorn St 38 B3
Clepington St 39 F1
Cobden Pl 38 A2
Cobden St 38 A2
Colinton Pl 38 A3
Commercial 39 F4
  St
Constitution 38 D3
  Rd
Constitution 38 D3
  St
Constitution 38 D3
  Ter
Corso St 38 B5

Cotton Rd 39 F2
Coupar St 38 A2
Courthouse 38 D3
  Sq
Court St 39 G1
Coutties Wynd 39 E5
Cowan St 39 G2
Cowgate 39 F4
Craigie St 39 H2
Crescent La 39 G3
Crescent St 39 G3
Crichton St 39 F5
Cross La 38 D5
Cross Row 38 D5
Cunningham 39 G2
  St

D

Dalfield Ct 39 E3
  Hilltown Ter
Daniel St 38 C4
Dens Brae 39 G3
Dens Rd 39 E1
Derby St 38 D1
Discovery 39 E6
  Quay
Dock St 39 F4
Dons Rd 39 E3
Douglas St 38 C4
Douglas Ter 38 C3
Drummond St 38 D2
Dudhope Ct 38 B3
Dudhope Cres 39 E3
  Rd
Dudhope St 39 E3
Dudhope Ter 38 C3
Dundonald St 39 F1
Dura St 39 G2
Dykehead Pl 39 G2

E

Eadies Rd 39 F3
Earl Grey Pl 39 F5
Eassons Angle 38 B4
East Dock St 39 G4
East Dock St 39 G3
  Retail Pk
East 38 D4
  Hendersons Wynd
East 39 F3
  Marketgait
East 38 D3
  Somerville Pl
Eastwell Rd 38 A1
East Whale La 39 G3
Edward St 38 C4
Eliza St 39 G1
Ellen St 39 F2
Elm St 38 A4
Erskine St 39 G2
Euclid Cres 39 E4
Euclid St 39 E4
Exchange St 39 F4

F

Fairbairn St 39 F1
Ferguson St 39 G3
Fingask St 38 D2
Fleuchar St 38 B4

Fords La 38 B5
  Perth Rd
Forebank Rd 39 F3
Forebank St 39 F3
  Forebank Rd
Forebank Ter 39 F3
  Forebank Rd
Forester St 39 E4
Forest Pk Pl 38 B4
Forest Pk Rd 38 B4
Forfar Rd 39 H1
Fort St 38 A5
Forum 39 E4
  Shop Cen
Foundry La 39 G3
Fraser St 38 D1
Fullarton St 38 A2
Fyffe St 38 B4

G

Gardners La 38 C3
Gardner St 38 A2
Garland Pl 38 D3
Gellatly St 39 F4
Glamis St 39 E2
Glenagnes Rd 38 A4
Glenagnes St 38 A4
Glenesk Av 38 B1
Glenisla Ter 38 B1
Gordon Sq 38 A2
Gordon St 38 A2
Gowrie St 38 B5
Graham Pl 39 G3
Greenbank Pl 38 A3
Greenfield Pl 38 C5
Greenmarket 39 E5
Guthrie St 38 D4

H

Harcourt St 38 D1
Harlow Pl 38 B1
Harriet St 39 G1
Hastings Pl 38 D1
Hawkhill 38 C5
Hawkhill Pl 38 C5
High Mill Ct 38 B6
High St 39 E5
Hillbank Gdns 39 F2
Hillbank Pl 39 F2
  Hillbank Rd
Hillbank Rd 39 F2
Hill Sq 39 E2
Hill St 38 D2
Hilltown 39 E2
Hilltown Ct 39 E3
  Hilltown Ter
Hilltown Ter 39 E3
Horsewater 38 D4
  Wynd
Horse Wynd 39 F4
Hunter St 38 D4
Hyndford Pl 38 A5
Hyndford St 38 A4

I

Inverary Ter 38 B2
Inverlaw Pl 38 C3
Inverlaw 38 C2
  Steps

Isla St 39 E1

J

Jamaica Sq 39 F2
  Ann St
Jamaica St 39 F2
Jamaica Twr 39 F2
  Alexander St
James St 39 E2
Janefield Pl 39 H1
Johnston St 38 D4

K

Keats Pl 38 D1
Kemback St 39 H2
Kenmore Ter 38 B2
Kennet Wk 39 E2
Kilberry St 38 A2
Killin Av 38 B2
Kincaldrum Pl 38 E2
Kincardine St 38 C5
Kinghorn Ct 38 D2
  Kinghorne Rd
Kinghorne Pl 38 D2
  Kinghorne Rd
Kinghorne Rd 38 C2
Kinghorne Ter 38 B3
Kinghorne Wk 38 D2
King St 39 F3
King William 39 F4
  St
Kinloch St 38 D2
Kinloch Ter 38 D2
Kinnaird St 38 D2
Kinpurnie Pl 38 B1
Kirk La 39 F3

L

Laburn St 39 E3
  Constitution Rd
Ladywell Av 39 F3
Laing Pl 39 F2
  Laing St
Laing St 39 F2
Lambs La 39 F2
Langlands St 39 G2
Larch St 38 C4
Laurel Bk 39 E3
Law Cres 38 B1
Lawrence St 38 B4
Law Rd 38 C2
Lawside Av 38 B3
Lawside Rd 38 B2
Lawside Ter 38 B2
Lawson Pl 38 D2
Law St 38 C2
Lawton Rd 38 C1
Lawton Steps 38 C1
Lawton Ter 38 C1
Leng St 38 D1
Lilybank Rd 39 H3
Lilybank Ter 39 H3
Lime St 38 A4
Lochee Rd 38 C3
Loganlee Ter 38 A3
Logie Av 38 A4
Logie Gdns 38 A4
Logie St 38 A2
Loons Rd 38 A2

Lorimer St 38 D1
Lower 38 C4
  Pleasance
Lynnewood Pl 39 H1
Lyon St 39 G2
Lytton St 38 B5

M
Macaulay St 38 D2
McDonald St 39 E3
McGill St 39 H2
McGonagall Sq 38 B6
  Patons La
McKinnon St 38 D2
McVicars La 38 C5
Magdalen Pl 38 C6
Magdalen Yd 38 B6
  Rd
Mains Rd 39 E1
Main St 39 E2
Maitland St 39 G2
Malcolms Penn 38 D4
Malcolm St 39 G2
Marine Par 39 G3
Martingale 39 G3
  Gdns
  Victoria Rd
Maryann La 39 F4
Maryfield Ter 39 H1
Mary Slessor 39 G3
  Sq
Maxwelltown 39 E2
  Twr
  Alexander St
Meadow Entry 39 F4
  Commercial St
Meadow La 39 F4
Meadow Pl 39 E3
  Bldgs
  Victoria Rd
Meadowside 39 E4
Melrose Ter 39 G1
Melville La 39 H3
Mid Rd 39 E1
Mid Wynd 38 C5
Millers Wynd 38 C5
Milnbank Rd 38 B4
Milnes E Wynd 38 C4
Miln St 38 D4
Milton St 38 D1
Minard Cres 38 C2
Minto Pl 38 A5
Mitchell St 38 B3
Molison St 39 G1
Morgan Pl 39 H2
Morgan St 39 H1
Mortimer St 38 D1
Murraygate 39 F4

N
Neish St 39 F1
Nelson St 39 F2
Nelson Ter 39 F3
  Nelson St
Nethergate 38 D5
New Inn Entry 39 E4
  High St
Nicoll St 39 E4
North Ellen St 39 F2
North Erskine 39 G2
  St

North George 39 E2
  St
North Isla St 39 F1
North Lindsay 39 E4
  St
North 38 D4
  Marketgait
North 38 D2
  Somerville Pl
North St 39 E1
North 39 F2
  Wellington St
North William 39 F2
  St

O
Ogilvie's Rd 39 E2
Ogilvie St 39 G2
Old Hawkhill 38 C5
Old Kings 38 A2
  Cross Rd
Osborne Pl 38 B6
Overgate Cen 39 E5

P
Palais Ct 39 E5
Panmure St 39 E4
Panmure Ter 38 D3
Paradise Rd 39 E3
Park Av 39 H2
Parker St 38 D3
Park Pl 38 D5
Park St 38 C4
Park Wynd 38 D5
Paterson St 38 D1
Patons La 38 B6
Patrick Pl 38 B6
Peddie St 38 A5
Peep O'day La 39 G3
Pennycook La 38 B5
Pentland Av 38 A3
Pentland Cres 38 A3
Perth Rd 38 C5
Peter St 39 F4
Pitfour St 38 A3
Pitkerro Rd 39 H1
Pleasance Ct 38 C4
  Douglas St
Polepark Rd 38 B4
Pole St 38 B4
Powrie Pl 39 E3
Princes St 39 G3
Prospect Pl 39 E3

Q
Queen St 39 F3

R
Raglan St 39 H2
Rankine St 38 B3
Rattray St 39 E4
Reform St 39 E4
Reid Sq 38 D1
  Reid St
Reid St 38 D2
Richmond Ter 38 A6
Ritchie's La 38 B5
  Hawkhill
Riverside Dr 38 D6
Robertson St 39 H3
Rockwell Pl 38 C1

Roseangle 38 C6
Rosebank Pl 39 E3
Rosebank Rd 39 E3
Rosebank St 39 E2
Rosebery St 38 B3
Rosefield St 38 B4
Rosemount Ter 38 D3
  Upper
  Constitution St
Royal Ex Ct 39 F4
  Commercial St
Royal Ex La 39 E4
  Meadowside
Russell Pl 38 D1
Ryehill La 38 B5

S
Saggar St 38 A3
St. Andrews 39 F4
  La
  St. Andrews St
St. Andrews 39 F4
  St
St. Davids La 38 D4
  West Marketgait
St. Mary Pl 38 B3
St. Mary St 38 C3
St. Matthews 39 H3
  La
St. Peter St 38 B5
St. Salvador St 39 E2
Salem St 39 E3
  Constitution Rd
Scott St 38 A4
Seabraes 38 D6
Seabraes Ct 38 D6
Seabraes La 38 D5
Seafield Cl 38 C6
Seafield La 38 C6
Seafield Rd 38 C6
Seagate 39 F4
Session St 38 D4
Seymour Av 38 A5
Seymour St 38 A4
Shaftesbury Pk 38 A5
Shaftesbury Pl 38 A5
Shaftesbury 38 A5
  Rd
Shaftesbury 38 A5
  Ter
Shelley Gdns 38 D1
Shepherds Ln 38 B5
Shore Ter 39 F4
  Castle St
Sibbald St 39 F1
Smalls La 38 D5
Smalls Wynd 38 D5
Soap Wks La 39 E3
Somerville Pl 38 D3
South Baffin 39 H3
  St
South George 39 F3
  St
South 39 F5
  Marketgait
South Tay St 38 D5
South Victoria 39 G4
  Dock Rd
South Ward 39 E4
  Rd
Speed St 38 A5

Spinners Wynd 38 B6
  Taylors La
Springfield 38 C5
Stephen's Yd 38 B6
Step Row 38 B6
Stirling Av 38 D2
Stirling St 38 D2
Stirling Ter 38 D2
Stobswell Rd 39 G1
Strathmartine 38 D1
  Rd
Strathmore Av 38 B1
Strathmore St 39 F1
Strawberry Bk 38 B5
Sugarhouse 39 F3
  Wynd

T
Taits La 38 B5
Tannadice Ct 39 F1
  Tannadice St
Tannadice St 39 E1
Tayfield Pl 38 B6
Taylors La 38 B6
Tay Rd Br 39 G5
Tay Sq 39 E5
Tay St La 39 E5
Temple La 38 D5
Thistle St 39 E1
Thomson St 38 C6
Timber St 39 G4
Trades La 39 F4
Tullideph Pl 38 A2
Tullideph Rd 38 A2
Tullideph St 38 A3
Tulloch Ct 39 E3
  Hilltown Ter

U
Union Pl 38 B5
Union St 39 E5
Union Ter 38 D3
Upper 38 D2
  Constitution St
Ure St 38 C5
Urquhart St 38 C4

V
Victoria Rd 39 E3
Victoria St 39 G3

W
Walker's Mill 39 F1
Walton St 38 C4
Ward Rd 38 D4
Watsons La 38 C4
  Hawkhill
Watson St 39 H3
Weavers Yd 39 G3
Wellbank La 38 A1
Wellgate Cen 39 F3
Wellington Sq 39 F3
  Ann St
Wellington St 39 F2
Wellington Twr 39 F2
  Alexander St
Well Rd 38 C5
West Bell St 38 D4
Westfield Av 38 C5
Westfield La 38 C6

Westfield Pl 38 C6
West 38 D4
  Hendersons Wynd
West Lyon St 39 G2
West 38 D4
  Marketgait
West Port 38 D5
West 38 D3
  Somerville Pl
West St 38 D1
West Victoria 39 G4
  Dock Rd
West Wf Rd 39 G4
West Wynd 38 C5
Wetherby Pl 38 C1
Whistler's Way 39 E3
  Ann St
Whitehall Cres 39 E5
Whitehall St 39 E5
Wilkies La 38 C4
William 39 E3
  Barclay Sq
William St 39 F2
Willison St 39 E4
Windsor Pl 38 B6
  Magdalen Yd Rd
Windsor St 38 A5
Windsor Ter 38 A5
Wishart St 38 D2
  Stirling Ter
Wolseley St 39 G1

Y
Yeaman Shore 39 E5
  Union St

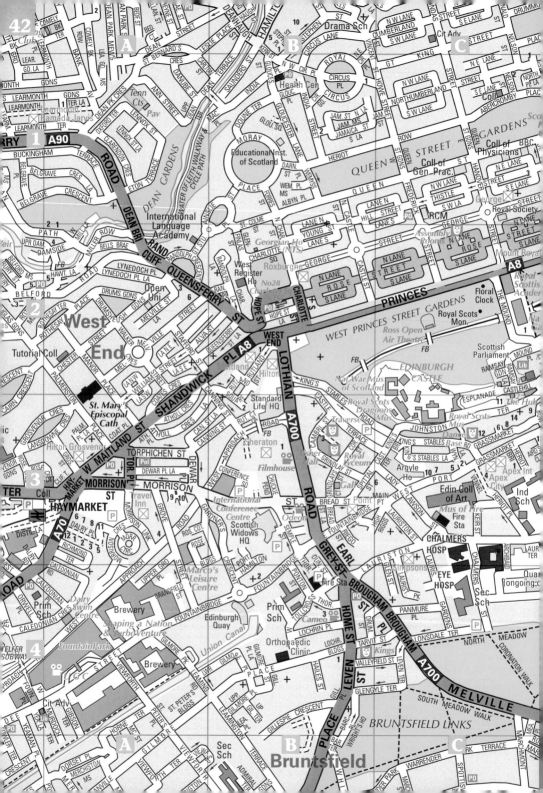

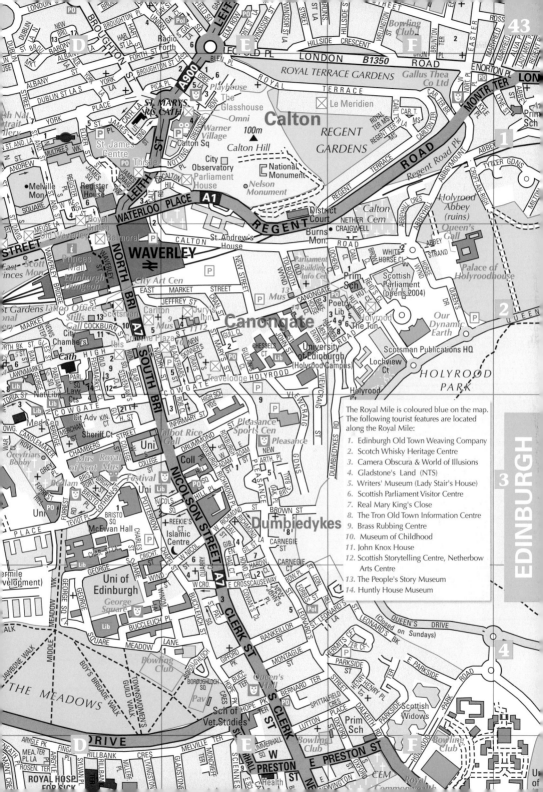

EDINBURGH

The Royal Mile is coloured blue on the map.
The following tourist features are located
along the Royal Mile:

1. Edinburgh Old Town Weaving Company
2. Scotch Whisky Heritage Centre
3. Camera Obscura & World of Illusions
4. Gladstone's Land (NTS)
5. Writers' Museum (Lady Stair's House)
6. Scottish Parliament Visitor Centre
7. Real Mary King's Close
8. The Tron Old Town Information Centre
9. Brass Rubbing Centre
10. Museum of Childhood
11. John Knox House
12. Scottish Storytelling Centre, Netherbow
    Arts Centre
13. The People's Story Museum
14. Huntly House Museum

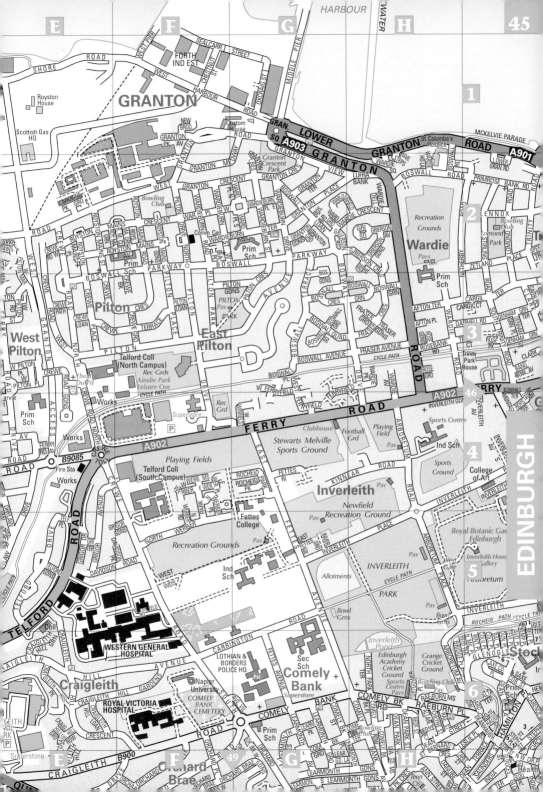

LEITH DOCKS

Britannia
Britannia Visitor Centre

IMPERIAL DOCK

Works

Depot

Depot

Depot

Depot

Works

1

2

EDINBURGH DOCK

Ocean Point One

PRINCE OF WALES

Holiday Inn Express

VICTORIA DOCK

Scottish Executive

OCEAN DRIVE

Malmaison

Custom Ho

ALBERT DOCK

Scot FM

Casino

CONS PL

Works

EDINBURGH

COMMERCIAL STREET

A199

BERNARD ST

BALTIC ST

SALAMANDER

A199

ALBERT ROAD

CARRON PL

STREET

SEAFIELD

MARINE ESPLANADE

3

Depot

Sewage

LEITH

EDINBURGH BUS. CEN

Prim Sch

LINKS GARDENS

Bowling Club

Pav

SEAFIELD CEMETERY AND CREMATORIUM

ROAD

JUNCTION STREET

CONSTITUTION

Prim Sch

Stevenson Coll
Queen Margaret University Coll
(Leith Campus)

LEITH LINKS

Gladstone

CLAREMONT PARK

Bowling Club

CLAREMONT GDNS

Allot

SEAFIELD

4

EASTERN GENERAL HOSPITAL

WALK

A900

LEITH

Depot

HERMITAGE

INDUSTRIAL RD

BURNS ST

VANBURGH PL

Prim Sch

RESTALRIG TER

CORNHILL TERRACE

RYEHILL

Spec Sch

PROSPECT BK

HERMITAGE

CYCLE PATH

RESTALRIG

South Leith

QUARRYHOLE PARK

HERMITAGE PARK

Prim Sch

Medical Centre

FINDLAY

5

CRAIG

GO

Craige

Sec Sch

Allot

Nisbet Ct

Hawkhill Ct

RESTALRIG

FINDLAY AVENUE

EASTERN CEMETERY

HAWKHILL AVENUE

LOCHEND ROAD

LOCHEND AVENUE

SLEIGH DRIVE

SLEIGH GDNS

Restalrig

Restalrig House

Prim Sch

Comm Cen

6

Prim Sch

Hillside

ALLANFIELD

Royal Mail Sorting Office

ALBION ROAD

John Cotton Bus. Cen

ALBION GDNS

Albion Business Centre

Lochend Loch

Lochend Ho

LOCHEND PARK

LOCHEND QUADRANT

MARIONVILLE ROAD

MARIONVILLE GRO

LOGANLEA

Prim Sch

LOGANLEA PLACE

Meadowbank Shopping Centre

Plaque Kiln

Castle Barns

ELGIN STREET

B1350

Bowling Club

LONDON ROAD

Abbeyhill

Meadowbank Sports Centre & Stadium

MONTGOMERY

Jock's

EDINBURGH

E   F   G   H

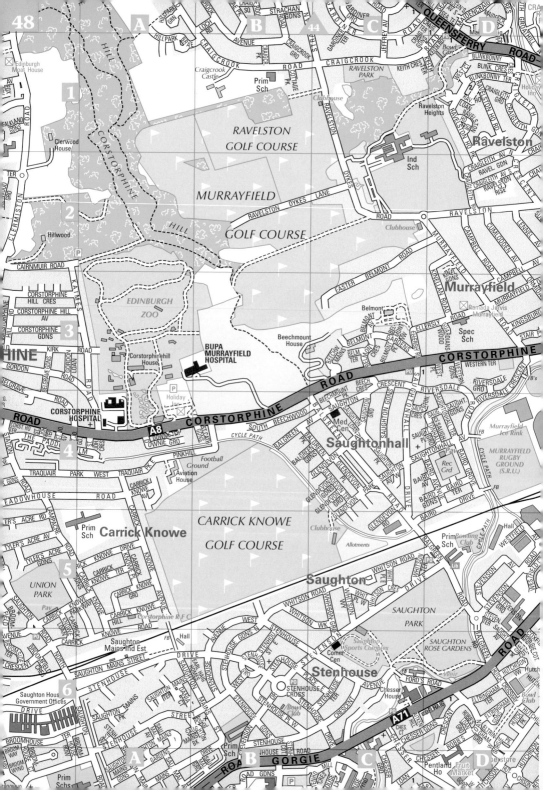

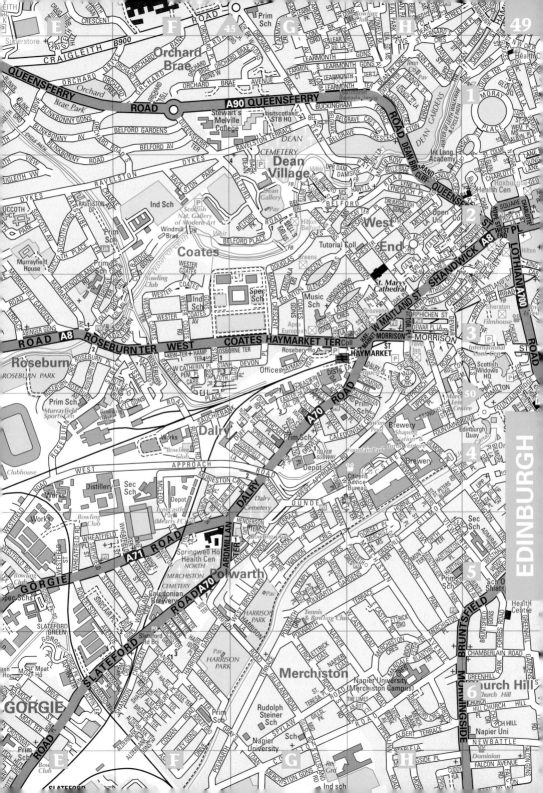

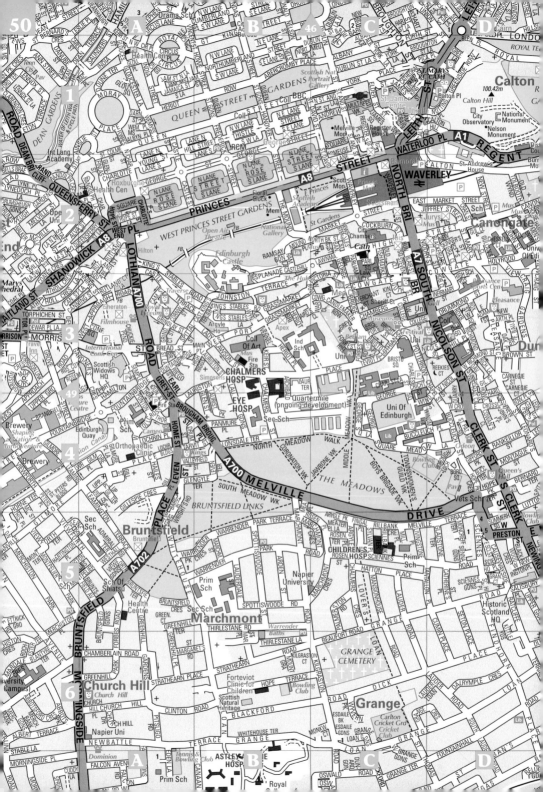

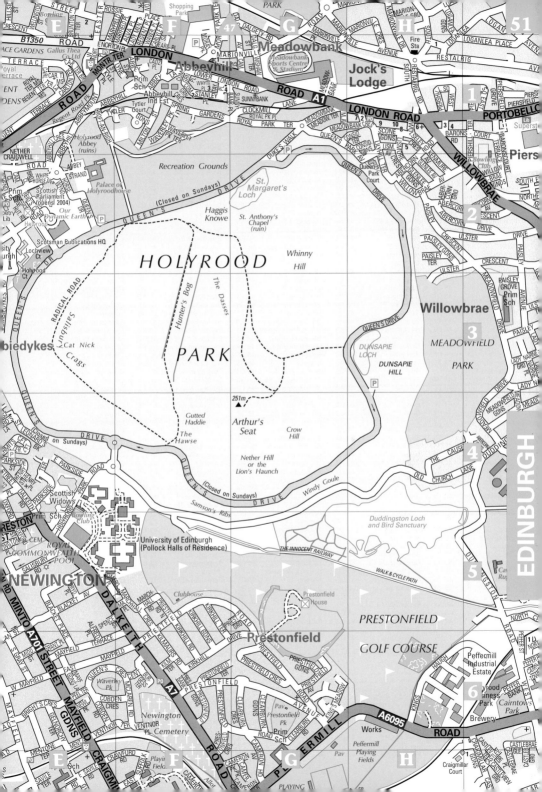

INDEX TO STREETS

Note: There are street names in this index which are followed by a number in **bold**. These numbers can be found on the map where there is insufficient space to show the street name in full.

A

Abbeyhill	43 F2	
Abbeyhill Cres	43 F2	
Abbeyhill Ind Est	51 F1	
Abbey La	51 F1	
Abbeymount	43 F1	
Abbey Strand	43 F2	
Abbey St	51 F1	
Abbotsford Ct	49 H6	
Abbotsford Cres	49 H6	
Abbotsford Pk	49 H6	
Abercorn Cres	51 H2	
Abercorn Dr	51 H2	
Abercorn Gro	51 H2	
Abercorn Rd	51 H2	
Abercromby Pl	42 C1	
Abinger Gdns	49 E3	
Academy Pk	47 F4	
Academy St	47 F4	
Admiral Ter	50 A5	
Admiralty St	47 E2	
Advocates Cl **1**	43 D2	
Afton Pl	45 H3	
Afton Ter	45 H3	
Agnew Ter	46 C3	
Ainslie Pl	42 A1	
Aird's Cl	42 C3	
Airlie Pl	46 B6	
Aitkenhill	48 C6	
Albany La	43 D1	
Albany St	43 D1	
Albany St La	43 D1	
Albert Dock	47 F2	
Albert Pl	46 D6	
Albert Rd	47 G3	
Albert St	47 E5	
Albert Ter	49 H6	
Albion	47 F6	
Business Cen		
Albion Gdns	47 F6	
Albion Pl	47 F6	
Albion Rd	47 F6	
Albion Ter	47 F6	
Albyn Pl	42 B1	
Alderbank Gdns	49 F6	
Alderbank Pl	49 F6	
Alderbank Ter	49 F6	
Alemoor Cres	47 G5	
Alemoor Pk	47 G5	
Alexander Dr	49 E5	
Alfred Pl	51 E5	
Allanfield	47 E6	
Allan St	45 H6	
Almondbank Ter	49 F6	
Alvanley Ter **1**	50 A5	
Alva Pl	51 F1	
Alva St	42 A2	
Anchor Cl **11**	43 D2	
Anchorfield	46 C2	
Anderson Pl	46 D3	
Andrew Wd Ct	46 B2	
Angle Pk Ter	49 G5	
Annandale St	46 C5	
Annandale St La	46 C5	
Annfield	46 C2	
Annfield St	46 C2	
Ann St	42 A1	
Antigua St **1**	46 D6	
Appin Ter	49 E6	
Arboretum Av	45 H6	
Arboretum Pl	45 H5	
Arboretum Rd	45 H4	
Archibald Pl	42 C3	
Arden St	50 B5	
Ardmillan Pl	49 G5	
Ardmillan Ter	49 F5	
Ardmillan Ter La **1**	49 F5	
Argyle Pk Ter	50 C5	
Argyle Pl	50 C5	
Argyle St	46 D2	
Argyll Ter **2**	42 A3	
Arthur St	47 E5	
Arthur St La	47 E5	
Ashley Gro	49 F6	
Ashley Pl	46 D4	

Ashley Ter	49 F6	
Ashville Ter	47 G5	
Assembly St	47 F3	
Atholl Cres	42 A3	
Atholl Cres La	42 A3	
Atholl Pl	42 A3	
Atholl Ter **3**	42 A3	
Auchinleck Ct	46 C2	
Auchinleck's	46 B2	
Brae **1**		
Avenue Vil	45 G6	
Avondale Pl	46 A6	

B

Back Dean	49 G2	
Baird Av	48 D4	
Baird Dr	48 C5	
Baird Gdns	48 D4	
Baird Gro	48 D4	
Baird Ter	48 D4	
Bakehouse Cl	43 E2	
Baker's Pl **1**	46 A6	
Balbirnie Pl	49 F3	
Balfour Pl	46 D5	
Balfour St	47 E4	
Balgreen Av	48 B4	
Balgreen Gdns	48 B4	
Balgreen Pk	48 B4	
Balgreen Rd	48 C4	
Ballantyne La **1**	47 E3	
Ballantyne Rd	47 E3	
Balmoral Pl	46 A6	
Baltic St	47 F3	
Bangholm Av	46 A3	
Bangholm	46 A3	
Bower Av		
Bangholm Gro	46 B3	
Bangholm Ln	46 B3	
Bangholm Pk	46 A3	
Bangholm Pl	46 A3	
Bangholm Rd	46 A3	
Bangholm Ter	46 A4	
Bangholm Vw	46 B3	
Bangor Rd	46 D3	
Bank St	43 D2	
Barclay Pl	42 B4	
Barclay Ter	50 A5	
Baronscourt Rd	51 H1	
Barony Pl **3**	46 C6	
Barony St	46 C6	
Barrie's Cl **14**	43 D2	
Bathfield	46 D2	
Bath Rd	47 G3	
Baxter's Pl **1**	43 E1	
Beaufort Rd	50 C6	
Beaverbank	46 B5	
Business Pk		
Beaverbank Pl	46 C5	
Beaverhall Rd	46 C5	
Bedford Ct	45 H6	
Bedford St	45 H6	
Beechmount Cres	48 C3	
Beechmount Pk	48 C3	
Beechwood Mains	48 C3	
Beechwood Ter	47 G5	
Belford Br	49 G2	
Belford Gdns	49 F1	
Belford Ms	49 G2	
Belford Pk	49 G2	
Belford Pl	49 F2	
Belford Rd	49 G2	
Belford Ter **1**	49 G2	
Belgrave Cres	49 G1	
Belgrave Cres La	49 G1	
Belgrave Ms	49 G1	
Belgrave Pl	49 G1	
Bellevue	46 C6	
Bellevue Cres	46 C6	
Bellevue Gdns	46 C6	
Bellevue Gro	46 C6	
Bellevue La	46 C6	
Bellevue Pl	46 C6	
Bellevue Rd	46 C6	
Bellevue St	46 C6	
Bellevue Ter	46 C5	

Bell Pl	46 A6	
Bells Brae	42 A2	
Bell's Mills	49 G2	
Bell's Wynd **2**	43 D2	
Belmont Av	48 C3	
Belmont Cres	48 C3	
Belmont Gdns	48 C3	
Belmont Pk	48 C3	
Belmont Ter	48 C3	
Belmont Vw	48 C3	
Belvedere Pk	46 B2	
Beresford Av	46 B2	
Beresford Gdns	46 B3	
Beresford Pl	46 A3	
Beresford Ter	46 A3	
Bernard St	47 F2	
Bernard Ter	43 E4	
Birnies Ct	44 B3	
Blackadder Pl	45 F2	
Blacket Av	51 E5	
Blacket Pl	51 E5	
Blackford Rd	50 B6	
Blackfriars St	43 E2	
Blackie Rd	47 G4	
Blackwood Cres	50 D5	
Blair St	43 D2	
Blandfield	46 C5	
Blantyre Ter	49 H6	
Bleachfield	46 C4	
Blenheim Pl	43 E1	
Blinkbonny Av	49 E1	
Blinkbonny Cres	48 D1	
Blinkbonny Gdns	49 E1	
Blinkbonny Gro	49 E1	
Blinkbonny Gro W	49 E1	
Blinkbonny Rd	49 E1	
Blinkbonny Ter	48 D1	
Boat Grn	46 B5	
Bonar Pl	46 C3	
Bonnington Av	46 C3	
Bonnington Gait **1**	46 D4	
Bonnington Gro	46 C3	
Bonnington	46 D4	
Ind Est		
Bonnington Rd	46 D4	
Bonnington Rd La	46 D4	
Bonnington Ter	46 C3	
Bonnyhaugh	46 C4	
Bonnyhaugh La	46 C4	
Boothacre Cotts **2**	47 H4	
Boothacre La	47 H4	
Boroughloch	43 E4	
Boroughloch Sq	43 E4	
Borthwick Pl	49 F3	
Borthwick's Cl **3**	43 D2	
Boswall Av	45 G3	
Boswall Cres	45 G3	
Boswall Dr	45 G2	
Boswall Gdns	45 G3	
Boswall Grn	45 H3	
Boswall Gro	45 G3	
Boswall Ln	45 G2	
Boswall Ms	45 G2	
Boswall Parkway	45 F2	
Boswall Pl	45 G2	
Boswall Quad	45 G3	
Boswall Rd	45 H2	
Boswall Sq	45 G3	
Boswall Ter	45 G3	
Bothwell St	47 E6	
Bowhill Ter	46 A4	
Bowie's Cl **1**	47 F3	
Bowling Grn, The	47 E3	
Bowling La **8**	47 E3	
Bowmont Pl	43 E4	
Boyd's Entry **2**	43 E2	
Boy's Brigade Wk	43 D4	
Brandfield St	42 A4	
Brandon St	46 B6	
Brandon Ter	46 B6	
Breadalbane St	46 D3	
Breadalbane Ter **5**	42 A3	
Bread St	42 B3	
Bread St La	42 B3	
Brewery La **2**	47 E3	
Briarbank Ter	49 F6	

Bridge Pl	45 H6	
Briery Bauks	43 E3	
Brighton St	43 D3	
Bright's Cres	51 E6	
Bright Ter **8**	42 A3	
Bristo Pl	43 D3	
Bristo Port	43 D3	
Bristo Sq	43 D3	
Broad Wynd **7**	47 F3	
Broomhouse Row	48 A6	
Brougham Pl	42 C4	
Brougham St	42 B4	
Broughton Mkt	46 C6	
Broughton Pl	46 C6	
Broughton Pl La	46 C6	
Broughton Rd	46 C5	
Broughton St	46 C6	
Broughton St La	43 D1	
Brown's Cl	43 F2	
Brown's Pl **4**	42 C3	
Brown St	43 E3	
Brown St La **8**	43 E3	
Brunswick Pl	46 D6	
Brunswick Rd	46 D6	
Brunswick St	46 D6	
Brunswick St La	46 D6	
Brunswick Ter **1**	47 E6	
Brunton Gdns **2**	47 E6	
Brunton Pl	47 E6	
Brunton Ter	47 E6	
Bruntsfield Av	50 A5	
Bruntsfield Cres	50 A5	
Bruntsfield Gdns	50 A5	
Bruntsfield Pl	49 H6	
Bruntsfield Ter	50 A5	
Bryson Rd	49 G5	
Buccleuch Pl	43 D4	
Buccleuch St	43 E4	
Buccleuch Ter	43 E4	
Buchanan St	47 E5	
Buckingham Ter	49 G1	
Bull's Cl **5**	43 F2	
Burgess St	47 F3	
Burgess Ter	51 F6	
Burlington St	47 E3	
Burns St	47 F4	

C

Cables Wynd	47 E3	
Cables Wynd Ho	47 E3	
Cadiz St	47 F3	
Cadzow Pl	51 F1	
Caithness Pl	46 A3	
Caledonian Cres	49 G4	
Caledonian Pl	42 A4	
Caledonian Rd	42 A3	
Calton Hill	43 E1	
Calton Rd	43 E2	
Calton Sq	43 E1	
Cambridge Av	46 D5	
Cambridge Gdns	46 D5	
Cambridge St	42 B3	
Cambridge St	42 B3	
La **3**		
Cambusnethan St	51 G1	
Cameron Ho Av	51 G6	
Campbell Av	48 D3	
Campbell Rd	48 D3	
Campbell's Cl	43 F2	
Candlemaker Row	43 D3	
Canning St	42 A2	
Canning St La	42 A3	
Cannon Wynd	46 D2	
Canon Ct **3**	46 B5	
Canongate	43 E2	
Canon La	46 B6	
Canonmills	46 B5	
Canonmills Br **2**	46 B5	
Canon St	46 B6	
Carberry Pl	49 F3	
Carfrae Gdns	44 B6	
Carfrae Gro	44 B6	
Carfrae Pk	44 B6	
Carfrae Rd	44 B6	
Cargil Ct	45 H3	
Cargil Ter	46 A3	

Carlton St	42 A1	
Carlton Ter	43 F1	
Carlton Ter Brae	43 F1	
Carlton Ter La	43 F1	
Carlton Ter Ms	43 F1	
Carlyle Pl	51 F1	
Carnegie Ct	43 E3	
Carnegie St	43 E3	
Caroline Pk Gro	45 F2	
Carpet La	47 F3	
Carrick Knowe	48 A4	
Ave		
Carrick Knowe	48 A5	
Gdns		
Carrick Knowe	48 A5	
Gro		
Carrick Knowe	48 A5	
Hill		
Carrick Knowe Pl	48 A5	
Carrick Knowe Ter	48 A5	
Carrington Rd	45 F6	
Carron Pl	47 G3	
Carrubber's Cl **5**	43 D2	
Casselbank St	47 E4	
Cassel's La	47 E4	
Castlehill	42 C2	
Castle St	42 B2	
Castle Ter	42 B3	
Castle Wynd N **11**	42 C3	
Castle Wynd S **6**	42 C3	
Cathcart Pl	49 G4	
Cathedral La	43 D1	
Catherine Pl	46 B5	
Causeway, The	51 H4	
Causewayside	50 D5	
Chalmers Bldgs **2**	42 B4	
Chalmers Cl **4**	43 E2	
Chalmers Cres	50 C5	
Chalmers St	42 C3	
Chamberlain Rd	50 A6	
Chambers St	43 D3	
Chancelot Cres	46 B3	
Chancelot Gro	46 B3	
Chancelot Ter	46 C3	
Chapel La **2**	47 F3	
Chapel St	43 E3	
Chapel Wynd **7**	42 C3	
Charlesfield **1**	43 D3	
Charles St	43 D3	
Charles St La	43 D3	
Charlotte La	42 B2	
Charlotte Sq	42 B2	
Chessels Ct	43 E2	
Chesser Av	48 C6	
Chesser Cotts **1**	48 D6	
Chesser Ct	48 C6	
Chesser Gdns	48 C6	
Chester St	42 A2	
Chestnut St	45 F1	
Cheyne St	45 H6	
Chuckie Pend	42 B3	
Church Hill	50 A6	
Church Hill Dr	50 A6	
Church Hill Pl	50 A6	
Circus Gdns	42 B1	
Circus La	46 A6	
Circus Pl	42 B1	
Citadel Ct	47 E2	
Citadel Pl	47 E2	
Citadel St **2**	47 E2	
Clarebank Cres	47 G4	
Claremont Bk	46 C6	
Claremont Ct	46 C5	
Claremont Cres	46 C5	
Claremont Gdns	47 G4	
Claremont Gro	46 C5	
Claremont Pk	47 G4	
Claremont Rd	47 G4	
Clarence St	46 A6	
Clarendon Cres	42 A1	
Clark Av	46 B3	
Clark Pl	46 A3	
Clark Rd	46 A3	
Clearburn Cres	51 G6	
Clearburn Gdns	51 G6	
Clearburn Rd	51 G6	

Clerk St 43 E4
Clifton Ter 42 A3
Clinton Rd 50 A6
Clockmill La 51 G1
Coalhill 47 E3
Coates Cres 42 A3
Coates Gdns 49 G3
Coates Pl 42 A3
Coatfield La 47 F3
Cobden Cres 51 E6
Cobden Rd 51 E6
Cobden Ter 7 42 A3
Coburg St 47 E3
Cochrane Pl 1 47 F4
Cochran Pl 46 C6
Cochran Ter 46 C6
Cockburn St 43 D2
Coffin La 49 G4
Coinyie Ho Cl 1 43 E2
College Wynd 2 43 D3
Collins Pl 46 A6
Coltbridge Av 49 E3
Coltbridge Gdns 49 F3
Coltbridge Millside 49 F3
Coltbridge Ter 49 E3
Coltbridge Vale 49 F3
Columba Av 44 C6
Columba Rd 44 C6
Colville Pl 46 A6
Comely Bk 45 G6
Comely Bk Av 45 H6
Comely Bk Gro 49 G1
Comely Bk Pl 45 H6
Comely Bk Pl Ms 2 45 H6
Comely Bk Rd 45 H6
Comely Bk Row 45 H6
Comely Bk St 45 G6
Comely Bk Ter 45 G6
Comely Grn Cres 51 F1
Comely Grn Pl 51 F1
Commercial St 47 E2
Commercial Wf 1 47 F2
Conference Sq 42 B3
Connaught Pl 46 C3
Considine Gdns 51 H1
Considine Ter 51 H1
Constitution Pl 47 F2
Constitution St 47 E2
Convening Ct 1 42 A2
Cooper's Cl 3 43 F2
Corbiehill Av 44 A5
Corbiehill Cres 44 A5
Corbiehill Gdns 44 B5
Corbiehill Gro 44 B5
Corbiehill Pk 44 A5
Corbiehill Pl 44 A5
Corbiehill Rd 44 A5
Corbiehill Ter 44 A5
Cornhill Ter 47 G4
Cornwallis Pl 46 B6
Cornwall St 42 B3
Coronation Wk 42 C4
Corstorphine Rd 48 B1
Corunna Pl 47 E3
Cottage Pk 48 B1
Couperfield 47 E3
Couper St 47 E2
Cowan Rd 49 F6
Cowan's Cl 43 E4
Cowgate 43 D3
Cowgatehead 43 D3
Coxfield 48 D6
Craigcrook Av 44 B6
Craigcrook Gdns 48 C1
Craigcrook Gro 48 B1
Craigcrook Pk 48 B1
Craigcrook Pl 1 44 D6
Craigcrook Rd 48 C1
Craigcrook Sq 44 B6
Craigcrook Ter 44 C6
Craighall Av 46 B2
Craighall Bk 46 B2
Craighall Cres 46 B2
Craighall Gdns 46 B3

Craighall Rd 46 B2
Craighall Ter 46 B3
Craigleith Av N 48 D2
Craigleith Av S 48 D2
Craigleith Bk 48 D1
Craigleith Cres 48 D1
Craigleith Dr 48 D1
Craigleith Gdns 48 D1
Craigleith Gro 48 D1
Craigleith Hill 49 E1
Craigleith Hill Av 48 D1
Craigleith Hill Cres 45 E6
Craigleith Hill Gdns 45 E6
Craigleith Hill Grn 45 E6
Craigleith Hill Gro 45 E6
Craigleith Hill Ln 45 E6
Craigleith Hill Pk 45 E6
Craigleith Hill Row 45 E6
Craigleith Retail Pk 45 E6
Craigleith Ri 48 D2
Craigleith Rd 49 E1
Craigleith Vw 48 D2
Craigroyston Gro 44 B4
Craigroyston Pl 44 B3
Cranston St 43 E2
Crarae Av 49 E2
Crawford Br 1 47 F6
Crewe Bk 45 F3
Crewe Cres 45 F3
Crewe Gro 45 F3
Crewe Ln 45 E3
Crewe Path 45 E3
Crewe Pl 45 E3
Crewe Rd Gdns 45 E3
Crewe Rd N 45 E3
Crewe Rd S 45 E4
Crewe Rd W 45 E3
Crewe Ter 45 E3
Crewe Toll 45 E4
Crichton's Cl 4 43 E2
Crichton St 43 D3
Crighton Pl 47 E5
Croall Pl 46 D6
Croft-an-righ 43 F1
Cromwell Pl 47 E2
Crown Pl 47 E4
Crown St 47 E4
Cumberland St 46 B6
Cumberland St N E La
Cumberland St N W La 46 B6
Cumberland St S E La
Cumberland St S W La 46 B6
Cumin Pl 50 D5
Cumlodden Av 48 D2
Cunningham Pl 1 47 E4

D
Daisy Ter 3 49 F6
Dalgety Av 47 G6
Dalgety Rd 47 G6
Dalgety St 51 G1
Dalkeith Rd 43 F4
Dalmeny Rd 46 C3
Dalmeny St 47 E5
Dalrymple Cres 50 D6
Dalry Pl 42 A3
Dalry Rd 49 G3
Dalziel Pl 1 51 F1
Damside 49 G2
Dania Ct 48 A6
Danube St 42 A1
Darnaway St 42 B1
Darnell Rd 45 H3
Davidson Gdns 44 B5
Davidson Pk 45 E5
Davidson Rd 45 E5
Davie St 43 E3
Dean Bk La 46 A6
Dean Br 42 A1

Deanery Cl 1 51 H1
Deanhaugh St 46 A6
Dean Pk Cres 42 A1
Dean Pk Ms 45 H6
Dean Pk St 45 H6
Dean Path 49 G1
Dean Path Bldgs 2 42 A2
Dean St 45 H6
Dean Ter 42 A1
Delhaig 48 D6
Denham Grn Av 46 A3
Denham Grn Pl 46 A3
Denham Grn Ter 46 A3
Derby St 46 C2
Devon Pl 49 G3
Dewar Pl 42 A3
Dewar Pl La 42 A3
Dick Pl 50 C6
Dicksonfield 46 D6
Dickson's Cl 5 43 E2
Dickson St 47 E5
Distillery La 49 G3
Dock Pl 47 E2
Dock St 47 E2
Dorset Pl 49 H5
Douglas Cres 49 G2
Douglas Gdns 49 G2
Douglas Gdns Ms 3 49 G2
Douglas Ter 1 42 A3
Doune Ter 42 B1
Downfield Pl 49 G4
Downie Gro 48 A4
Downie Ter 48 A4
Drumdryan St 42 B4
Drummond Pl 46 B6
Drummond St 43 E3
Drumsheugh Gdns 42 A2
Drumsheugh Pl 3 42 A2
Drum Ter 47 F6
Dryden Gait 46 D5
Dryden Gdns 46 D5
Dryden Pl 51 E5
Dryden St 46 D5
Dryden Ter 46 D5
Drylaw Av 44 D6
Drylaw Cres 44 C6
Drylaw Gdns 44 C5
Drylaw Grn 44 C6
Drylaw Gro 44 C6
Drylaw Ho Gdns 44 C5
Drylaw Ho Paddock 44 C5
Dublin Meuse 43 D1
Dublin St 46 C6
Dublin St La N 46 C6
Dublin St La S 43 D1
Dudley Av 46 C2
Dudley Av S 46 D3
Dudley Bk 46 C2
Dudley Cres 46 C2
Dudley Gdns 46 C2
Dudley Gro 46 C2
Dudley Ter 46 C2
Duff Rd 49 G4
Duff St 49 G4
Duff St La 49 G4
Duke Pl 47 F4
Duke St 47 F4
Duke's Wk 51 G2
Dumbiedykes Rd 43 F3
Dunbar St 42 B3
Duncan Pl 47 F4
Duncan St 50 D6
Dundas St 46 B6
Dundee St 49 G4
Dundee Ter 49 G5
Dundonald St 46 B6
Dunedin St 46 C5
Dunlop's Ct 12 43 C3
Dunrobin Pl 46 A6

E
Earl Grey St 42 B3
Earl Haig Gdns 46 A3

Earl Haig Homes 48 B6
Earlston Pl 51 F1
East Adam St 43 E3
East Broughton Pl 1 46 C6
East Castle Rd 49 H5
East Claremont St 46 C6
East Ct 2 48 D1
East Cromwell St 47 E2
East Crosscauseway 43 E4
Easter Belmont Rd 48 C3
Easter Dalry Dr 49 G3
Easter Dalry Pl 1 49 G3
Easter Dalry Rigg 3 49 G4
Easter Dalry Rd 49 G3
Easter Dalry Wynd 49 G3
Easter Drylaw Av 44 D5
Easter Drylaw Bk 44 D4
Easter Drylaw Dr 44 D5
Easter Drylaw Gdns 44 D5
Easter Drylaw Gro 44 D5
Easter Drylaw Ln 44 D4
Easter Drylaw Pl 44 D5
Easter Drylaw Vw 44 D5
Easter Drylaw Way 44 D5
Easter Hermitage 47 G5
Easter Rd 47 E6
Easter Warriston 46 B4
East Fettes Av 45 G5
East Fountainbridge 42 B3
East Hermitage Pl 47 F4
East Lillypot 46 A3
East London St 46 C6
East Mkt St 43 D2
East Mayfield 51 E6
East Montgomery Pl 47 E6
East Newington Pl 50 D5
East Norton Pl 43 F1
East Parkside 50 D5
East Preston St 50 D5
East Preston St La 3 50 D5
East Restalrig Ter 47 G4
East Sciennes St 50 D5
East Scotland St La 46 C6
East Silvermills La 46 A6
East Trinity Rd 46 A3
East Werberside 45 H4
East Werberside Pl 45 H4
Edina Pl 47 E6
Edina St 47 E6
Edinburgh Dock 47 G2
Eglinton Cres 49 G3
Eglinton St 3 49 F3
Eildon St 46 B5
Eildon Ter 46 A5
Elbe St 47 F3
Elder St 43 D1
Elder St E 5 43 D1
Elgin Pl 49 G3
Elgin St 47 E6
Elgin St N 47 E6
Elgin Ter 47 E6
Elizafield 46 D4
Ellersly Rd 48 C3
Elliot St 47 E6
Elm Pl 2 47 G4
Elm Row 46 D6
Elmwood Ter 47 G4
Eltringham Gdns 48 D6
Eltringham Gro 48 D6
Eltringham Ter 48 D6
Esdaile Bk 50 C6
Esdaile Gdns 50 C6
Esdaile Pk 1 50 C6
Esplanade 42 C3
Eton Ter 42 A1
Ettrickdale Pl 46 A5
Ettrick Gro 49 H5
Ettrick Ln 49 G6

Ettrick Rd 49 G6
Eyre Cres 46 B6
Eyre Pl 46 B6
Eyre Ter 46 B6

F
Falcon Gdns 50 A6
Ferryfield 45 G4
Ferry Rd 46 C3
Ferry Rd Av 45 E4
Ferry Rd Dr 45 E3
Ferry Rd Gdns 44 D4
Ferry Rd Gro 44 D4
Ferry Rd Pl 44 D4
Festival Sq 1 42 B3
Fettes Av 45 G6
Fettes Ri 45 G4
Fettes Row 46 B6
Fidra Ct 44 B3
Findhorn Pl 50 D5
Findlay Av 47 H5
Findlay Cotts 47 H5
Findlay Gdns 47 H5
Findlay Gro 47 H5
Findlay Medway 47 H5
Fingal Pl 50 C5
Fingzies Pl 3 47 F4
Fishmarket Sq 2 46 C1
Fleshmarket Cl 13 43 D2
Forbes Rd 50 A6
Forbes St 43 E4
Ford's Rd 48 C6
Forres St 42 B1
Forrest Hill 43 D3
Forrest Rd 43 D3
Forth Ind Est 45 F1
Fort Ho 46 D2
Forth St 43 D1
Forthview Rd 44 D6
Forthview Ter 44 C6
Fountainbridge 42 B4
Fowler Ter 49 G5
Fox St 47 G3
Fraser Av 45 H3
Fraser Cres 45 H3
Fraser Gdns 45 H3
Fraser Gro 45 H3
Frederick St 42 C1

G
Gabriel's Rd 6 43 D1
Gabriel's Rd (Stockbridge) 6 46 A6
Gardiner Gro 44 C6
Gardiner Rd 44 C6
Gardiner Ter 48 C1
Gardner's Cres 42 A3
Garscube Ter 49 E2
Gayfield Cl 46 D6
Gayfield Pl 46 D6
Gayfield Pl La 46 D6
Gayfield Sq 46 D6
Gayfield St 46 C6
Gayfield St La 46 C6
Gentle's Entry 8 43 F2
George IV Br 43 D2
George Sq 43 D4
George Sq La 43 D4
George St 42 B2
Gibbs Entry 43 E3
Gibson St 46 D4
Gibson Ter 42 A4
Gifford Pk 43 E4
Giles St 47 E3
Gillespie Cres 42 B4
Gillespie Pl 42 B4
Gillespie St 42 B4
Gillsland Pk 49 G6
Gillsland Rd 49 G6
Gilmore Pk 42 A4
Gilmore Pl 49 H5
Gilmore Pl La 42 B4
Gilmour's Entry 7 43 E3
Gilmour St 43 E3
Gladstone Pl 47 G4

EDINBURGH

Gladstone Ter	50	D5
Glanville Pl 5	46	A6
Glencairn Cres	49	G3
Glendevon Av	48	C4
Glendevon Gdns	48	C4
Glendevon Gro	48	C4
Glendevon Pk	48	C5
Glendevon Pl	48	C4
Glendevon Rd	48	C5
Glendevon Ter	48	C4
Glenfinlas St	42	B2
Glengyle Ter	42	B4
Glenlea Cotts	48	D6
Glenlee Av	51	H2
Glenlee Gdns	51	H2
Glenogle Ct	46	A5
Glenogle Pl 7	46	A5
Glenogle Rd	46	A5
Glenogle Ter	46	A5
Glenorchy Pl 4	43	E1
Glenorchy Ter	51	E6
Glen St	42	C3
Gloucester La	42	B1
Gloucester Pl	42	B1
Gloucester Sq	42	B1
Gloucester St	42	B1
Goldenacre Ter	46	A4
Gordon St	47	F4
Gorgie Cotts	48	D6
Gorgie Pk Cl	49	E6
Gorgie Pk Rd	49	E5
Gorgie Rd	49	E5
Gosford Pl	46	C3
Graham St	46	D3
Grandfield	46	B3
Grandville	46	B2
Grange Ct	50	D5
Grange Cres	50	C6
Grange Ln	50	B6
Grange Ln Gdns	50	C6
Grange Rd	50	C5
Granton Cres	45	G2
Granton Gdns	45	G2
Granton Gro	45	G2
Granton Mains Av	44	D2
Granton Mains Bk 1	44	D2
Granton Mains Brae	44	D2
Granton Mains Ct	45	E2
Granton Mains E	45	E2
Granton Mains Gait	44	D2
Granton Mains Vale	44	D2
Granton Mains Wynd	44	D2
Granton Medway	45	F2
Granton Mill Cres	44	D2
Granton Mill Dr	44	D2
Granton Mill March	44	C3
Granton Mill Pk	44	C3
Granton Mill Pl	44	C2
Granton Mill Rd	44	C2
Granton Mill W 1	44	C2
Granton Pk Av	45	F1
Granton Pl	45	G2
Granton Rd	45	G2
Granton Sq	45	G1
Granton Ter	45	G2
Granton Vw	45	G1
Grantully Pl	51	E6
Granville Ter	49	H5
Grassmarket	42	C3
Grays Ct 6	43	E3
Gray's Ln	49	F6
Great Junct St	47	E3
Great King St	42	C1
Great Michael Cl 4	46	C1
Great Michael Ri	46	C2
Great Michael Sq 1	46	C1
Great Stuart St	42	A2
Green, The	44	A4
Greendale Pk	44	B4
Greenhill Ct	50	A5
Greenhill Gdns	50	A5
Greenhill Pk	50	A6
Greenhill Pl	50	A6
Greenhill Ter	50	A5
Greenside End 6	43	E1
Greenside La	43	E1
Greenside Pl 5	43	E1
Greenside Row	43	E1
Green St	46	C6
Greyfriars Pl	43	D3
Grierson Av	45	H2
Grierson Cres	45	H2
Grierson Gdns	45	H2
Grierson Rd	45	G2
Grierson Sq	45	H2
Grierson Vil	45	H2
Grigor Av	45	E5
Grigor Dr	45	E5
Grigor Gdns	45	E5
Grigor Ter	45	E5
Grindlay St	42	B3
Grindlay St Ct	42	B3
Groathill Av	44	D6
Groathill Gdns E	44	D6
Groathill Gdns W	44	D6
Groathill Rd N	44	D5
Groathill Rd S	44	D6
Grosvenor Cres	49	G3
Grosvenor Gdns	49	G3
Grosvenor St	42	A3
Grove St	42	A3
Grove Ter 4	42	A3
Guardianswood	48	D3
Gullan's Cl	43	E2
Gunnet Ct	44	B3
Guthrie St	43	D3
Gypsy Brae	44	C2

H

Haddington Pl	46	D6
Haddon's Ct	43	E3
Hailes St	42	B4
Halmyre St	47	E5
Hamburgh Pl 1	46	D2
Hamilton Pl	46	A6
Hamilton's Folly Ms 5	43	E4
Hamilton Wynd	46	D2
Hammermen's Entry	43	E2
Hampton Pl 4	49	F3
Hampton Ter	49	F3
Hanover St	42	C1
Harden Pl	49	G5
Hardwell Cl	43	E4
Harrismith Pl	47	F6
Harrison Gdns	49	F6
Harrison La	49	G5
Harrison Pl	49	F6
Harrison Rd	49	F5
Hartington Gdns	50	A5
Hartington Pl	49	H5
Hart St	46	C6
Hart St La	46	C6
Hatton Pl	50	C5
Haugh St	46	A6
Hawkhill	47	G5
Hawkhill Av	47	F5
Hawkhill Ct	47	G5
Hawthornbank La	42	A2
Hawthornbank Pl	46	D2
Hawthornbank Ter 2	46	D2
Hawthorn Bldgs 2	49	G2
Hawthornden Pl	46	D5
Hawthorn Ter 5	42	A2
Hawthornvale	46	C2
Haymarket	42	A3
Haymarket Ter	49	G3
Haymarket Yards	49	G3
Hazelbank Ter	49	F6
Henderland Rd	49	E3
Henderson Gdns 4	47	E3
Henderson Pl	46	B6
Henderson Pl La	46	A6
Henderson Row	46	A6
Henderson St	47	E3
Henderson Ter	49	G5
Henry Pl	43	F4
Henry St	43	F4
Heriot Br	42	C3
Heriot Cross 1	42	C3
Heriot Hill Ter	46	B5
Heriot Pl	42	C3
Heriot Row	42	B1
Hermand Cres	49	F6
Hermand St	49	E6
Hermand Ter	49	E6
Hermitage Pk	47	G5
Hermitage Pk Gro	47	G5
Hermitage Pk Lea	47	G5
Hermitage Pk S	47	G5
Hermitage Pl	47	F4
Hermits Cft	43	F4
High Riggs	42	C3
High Sch Yards	43	E3
High St	43	D2
Hillend Pl 10	51	H1
Hillhouse Rd	44	A5
Hillpark Av	44	A5
Hillpark Brae	48	A1
Hillpark Ct	44	A5
Hillpark Cres	44	A6
Hillpark Dr	44	A5
Hillpark Gdns	44	A6
Hillpark Grn	44	A6
Hillpark Gro	44	A6
Hillpark Ln	44	B6
Hillpark Rd	44	A6
Hillpark Ter	44	A6
Hillpark Way	44	B6
Hillpark Wd	44	B6
Hill Pl	43	E3
Hillside Cres	46	D6
Hillside St	47	E6
Hill Sq	43	E3
Hill St	42	B1
Hill St La N	42	B1
Hill St La S	42	C2
Hillview	44	C6
Hollybank Ter	49	F6
Holyrood Ct	43	F2
Holyrood Pk	51	F2
Holyrood Pk Rd	51	E5
Holyrood Rd	43	E2
Home St	42	B4
Hopefield Ter	46	D2
Hope Pk Cres	43	E4
Hope Pk Sq 1	43	E4
Hope Pk Ter	43	E4
Hope St	42	B2
Hope St La	42	B2
Hope Ter	50	B6
Hopetoun Cres	46	D6
Hopetoun St	46	D6
Horne Ter	42	A4
Horse Wynd	43	F2
House o'Hill Av	44	B5
House o'Hill Brae	44	B5
House o'Hill Cres	44	B5
House o'Hill Gdns	44	C5
House o'Hill Grn	44	B5
House o'Hill Gro	44	B5
House o'Hill Pl	44	B5
House o'Hill Rd	44	B5
House o'Hill Row	44	C5
House o'Hill Ter	44	B5
Howard Pl	46	B5
Howard St	46	B5
Howden St	43	E3
Howe St	42	C1
Hugh Miller Pl	46	A6
Hunter's Cl 13	42	C3
Hunter Sq	43	D2
Huntingdon Pl	46	D6
Huntly St	46	B5
Hutchison Crossway	48	D6
Hutchison Ho	49	E6
Hutchison	49	E6
Hutchison Medway	48	D6
Hutchison Pk	48	D6
Hutchison Rd	49	E6
Hutchison Vw	48	D6
Hutton Cl	43	F2
Hutton Rd	43	F2

I

Imperial Dock	47	F1
Inchcolm Ct	44	D3
Inchgarvie Ct	45	E4
Inchkeith Ct	46	D5
Inchmickery Ct	44	B3
India Bldgs 3	43	D3
India Pl	42	B1
India St	42	B1
Industrial Rd	47	H4
Industry Home 1	46	D3
Industry La	46	D3
Infirmary St	43	E3
Inglis Ct 2	42	C3
Inverleith Av	46	A4
Inverleith Av S	46	A4
Inverleith Gdns	45	H4
Inverleith Gro	45	G5
Inverleith Pl	45	H4
Inverleith Pl La	46	A4
Inverleith Row	46	A4
Inverleith Ter	46	A5
Inverleith Ter La	46	A5
Iona St	47	E5
Ivy Ter	49	F5

J

Jackson's Entry 7	43	F2
Jamaica Ms	42	B1
Jamaica St	42	B1
Jamaica St N La	42	B1
Jamaica St S La	42	B1
Jamaica St W 2	42	B1
James' Ct 4	42	C3
James Craig Wk	43	D1
Jameson Pl	47	E5
Jane St	47	E4
Jane Ter 2	51	F1
Jawbone Wk	43	D4
Jeffrey Av	48	C1
Jeffrey St	43	D2
Jessfield Ter	46	C2
John Cotton Business Cen	47	F6
John's La	47	F3
John's Pl	47	F4
Johnston Ter	42	C3
Junction Pl	47	E4

K

Keir St	42	C3
Keith Cres	48	C1
Keith Row	48	D1
Keith Ter	48	D1
Kemp Pl	46	A6
Kenmure Av	51	H2
Kerr St	46	A6
Kew Ter	49	F3
Kilgraston Ct	50	B6
Kilgraston Rd	50	C6
Kilmaurs Rd	51	F6
Kilmaurs Ter	51	F6
Kincaid's Ct	43	D3
Kinellan Gdns	48	D3
Kinellan Rd	48	D2
Kinghorn Pl	46	C3
King's Br	42	C3
Kingsburgh Rd	48	D3
Kings Haugh	51	H6
King's Meadow	51	G6
King's Stables La	42	C3
King's Stables Rd	42	C3
King St	47	E3
Kinnear Rd	45	G4
Kirkgate	47	F3
Kirkhill Dr	51	F6
Kirkhill Gdns	51	F5
Kirkhill Rd	51	F5
Kirkhill Ter	51	F5
Kirk St	47	E4
Kirkwood Pl 3	43	F1
Kittle Yards	50	D5
Kyle Pl	43	F1

L

Ladehead	46	C4
Lady Lawson St	42	C3
Lady Menzies Pl	51	F1
Lady Stair's Cl 6	43	D2
Lady Wynd	42	C3
Lamb's Cl 2	43	E4
Lamb's Ct 1	46	B1
Lansdowne Cres	49	G3
Lapicide Pl	46	D3
Largo Pl	46	D3
Lauderdale St	50	B5
Lauder Ln	50	D6
Lauder Rd	50	C5
Laurel Ter 1	49	F5
Laurie St	47	F4
Lauriston Gdns	42	C3
Lauriston Pk	42	C3
Lauriston Pl	42	B4
Lauriston St	42	C3
Lauriston Ter	42	C3
Laverockbank Av	46	B2
Laverockbank Cres	46	B2
Laverockbank Gdns	46	B2
Laverockbank Gro	46	B2
Laverockbank Rd	46	B2
Laverockbank Ter	46	B2
Lawnmarket	43	D2
Leamington Pl	42	B4
Leamington Rd	42	A4
Leamington Ter	42	B4
Learmonth Av	45	G6
Learmonth Ct	49	G1
Learmonth Cres	49	G1
Learmonth Gdns	49	G1
Learmonth Gdns La	49	G1
Learmonth Gdns Ms	45	H6
Learmonth Gro	45	G6
Learmonth Pk	45	G6
Learmonth Pl	45	G6
Learmonth Ter	49	G1
Learmonth Ter La	49	G1
Learmonth Vw 1	42	A1
Leith Docks	47	E1
Leith Links	47	F4
Leith St	43	D1
Leith Wk	46	D6
Lennel Av	48	D2
Lennox Row	46	A2
Lennox St	42	A1
Lennox St La	42	A1
Leopold Pl	46	D6
Leslie Pl	45	H6
Leven Cl 1	42	B4
Leven St	42	B4
Leven Ter	42	C4
Lewis Ter 12	42	A3
Liddesdale Pl	46	A5
Lilyhill Ter	51	H1
Lily Ter 1	49	F6
Limes, The	49	H6
Lindean Pl	47	G4
Lindsay Pl	46	D2
Lindsay Rd	46	D2
Lindsay St	46	D2
Links Gdns	47	G3
Links Gdns La	47	G3
Links La 3	47	F3
Links Pl	47	F3
Linksview Ho	47	F3
Lismore Av	51	H1
Lismore Cres	51	H1
Little King St	43	D1
Livingstone Pl	50	C5

Name	Ref
Lixmount Av	46 B2
Lixmount Gdns	46 B2
Loaning Rd	47 H6
Lochend Av	47 G6
Lochend Castle Barns	47 G6
Lochend Cl	43 F2
Lochend Cres	47 H6
Lochend Dr	47 G6
Lochend Gdns	47 G6
Lochend Gro	47 H6
Lochend Pk	47 G6
Lochend Quad	47 H6
Lochend Rd	47 G5
Lochend Rd S	47 G6
Lochend Sq	47 G6
Lochrin Bldgs	42 B4
Lochrin Pl	42 B4
Lochrin Ter 3	42 B4
Loch Rd	44 B6
Lochview Ct	43 F2
Loganlea Dr	51 H1
Loganlea Gdns	47 H6
Logan St	46 B6
Logie Grn Gdns	46 B5
Logie Grn Ln	46 B5
Logie Grn Rd	46 B5
Logie Mill	46 B5
Lomond Rd	46 A2
London Rd	43 E1
London St	46 C6
Long Craig Rigg	44 D1
Long Craig Rd	44 D1
Lonsdale Ter	42 C4
Lord Russell Pl 1	50 D5
Lorne Pl	47 E5
Lorne Sq	47 E5
Lorne St	47 E5
Lothian Rd	42 B2
Lothian St	43 D3
Lovers' Ln	50 C5
Lower Gilmore Pl	42 A4
Lower Granton Rd	45 H2
Lower London Rd	51 F1
Lufra Bk	45 H2
Lutton Pl	43 E4
Lynedoch Pl	42 A2
Lynedoch Pl La	42 A2
Lyne St	51 F1

M

Name	Ref
McDonald Pl	46 C5
McDonald Rd	46 C5
McDonald St	46 D5
McKelvie Par	46 A1
Mackenzie Pl	42 B1
McLaren Rd	51 F6
McLaren Ter 11	42 A3
McLeod St	49 F4
McNeill St	42 A4
Madeira Pl	46 D3
Madeira St	46 D2
Magdala Cres	49 G3
Magdala Ms	49 G3
Maidencraig Ct	44 D6
Maidencraig Cres	44 D6
Maidencraig Gro	44 D6
Main Pt	42 C3
Main St	44 A5
Malta Grn 2	46 A6
Malta Ter	46 A6
Manderston St	47 E4
Manor Pl	42 A2
Mansfield Pl	46 C6
Mansionhouse Rd	50 C5
Marchfield Gro	44 B5
Marchfield Pk	44 A5
Marchfield Pk La	44 A5
Marchfield Ter	44 B6
March Gait	44 A6
March Gro	44 A6
Marchhall Cres	51 F5
Marchhall Pl	51 F5
Marchhall Rd	51 F5
Marchmont Cres	50 B5
Marchmont Rd	50 B5
Marchmont St	50 B5
March Pines	44 A6
March Rd	44 A6
Mardale Cres	49 H6
Marine Dr	44 B2
Marine Esplanade	47 H3
Marionville Av	47 G6
Marionville Cres	47 H6
Marionville Dr	47 H6
Marionville Gro	47 H6
Marionville Medway 1	47 H6
Marionville Pk	47 G6
Marionville Rd	51 F1
Marischal Pl 1	48 D1
Maritime La	47 F3
Maritime St	47 F3
Market St	43 D2
Marshall's Ct 3	43 E1
Marshall St 2	43 E3
Martello Ct	44 B3
Maryfield	43 F1
Maryfield Pl	51 F1
Mary's Pl 1	45 H6
May Ct	44 B3
Mayfield Gdns	51 E6
Mayfield Gdns La	51 E6
Mayfield Rd	51 E6
Mayfield Ter	51 E6
Mayville Gdns	46 B2
Mayville Gdns E	46 B2
Meadowbank	51 G1
Meadowbank Av	51 G1
Meadowbank Cres	51 G1
Meadowbank Ho	51 H1
Meadowbank Pl 7	51 H1
Meadow Bk Shop Pk	47 F6
Meadowbank Ter	51 G1
Meadow La	43 D4
Meadow Pl	42 C4
Meadow Pl La	50 C5
Melbourne Pl 7	43 D2
Melgund Ter	46 C6
Melville Cres	42 A2
Melville Dr	42 C4
Melville Pl 6	42 A2
Melville St	42 A2
Melville St La	42 A2
Melville Ter	50 C5
Mentone Gdns	51 E6
Merchant St	43 D3
Merchiston Av	49 H5
Merchiston Bk Av	49 H6
Merchiston Bk Gdns	49 H6
Merchiston Cres	49 H6
Merchiston Gro	49 H5
Merchiston Ms	49 H5
Merchiston Pk	49 H5
Merchiston Pl	49 H6
Mertoun Pl	49 G5
Meuse La	43 D2
Middleby St	51 E6
Middlefield	46 D5
Middle Meadow Wk	43 D4
Middle Pier	45 G1
Mid Gillsland Rd	49 G6
Millerfield Pl	50 C5
Miller Row	42 A2
Mill La	47 E3
Milnacre	46 C4
Milton St	51 F1
Minto St	51 E5
Mitchell St	47 F3
Moat Dr	49 E6
Moat Ho	49 E6
Moat Pl	49 E6
Moat St	49 E6
Moat Ter	49 E6
Moncrieff Ter	50 D5
Monkwood Ct	50 C6
Monmouth Ter	46 A3
Montague St	43 E4
Montagu Ter	46 A4
Montgomery St	46 D6
Montgomery St La	46 D6
Montpelier	49 H5
Montpelier Pk	49 H5
Montpelier Ter	49 H5
Montrose Ter	43 F1
Moray Pk	51 F1
Moray Pk Ter	51 F1
Moray Pl	42 B1
Morningside Rd	49 H6
Morrison Circ	42 A3
Morrison Cres	42 A3
Morrison Link	42 A3
Morrison St	42 A3
Moston Ter	51 E6
Mound, The	42 C2
Mound Pl	42 C2
Mount Gra	50 B6
Muirdale Ter 1	44 C6
Muirhouse Av	44 C4
Muirhouse Av N	44 C3
Muirhouse Bk	44 C4
Muirhouse Cl	44 B4
Muirhouse Ct	44 C3
Muirhouse Cres	44 C3
Muirhouse Dr	44 B3
Muirhouse Gdns	44 B3
Muirhouse Grn	44 C4
Muirhouse Gro	44 B3
Muirhouse Ln	44 C3
Muirhouse Medway	44 B3
Muirhouse Pk	44 B4
Muirhouse Parkway	44 C3
Muirhouse Pl E	44 C4
Muirhouse Pl W	44 C4
Muirhouse Ter	44 B4
Muirhouse Vw	44 B3
Muirhouse Way	44 C4
Mulberry Pl 1	46 C3
Multrees Wk	43 D1
Munro Pl 1	46 B5
Murano Pl	47 E6
Murdoch Ter	42 A4
Murieston Cres	49 F4
Murieston Cres La 2	49 G4
Murieston La	49 F4
Murieston Pl	49 F4
Murieston Rd	49 F4
Murieston Ter	49 F4
Murrayfield Av	49 E3
Murrayfield Dr	48 D3
Murrayfield Gdns	49 E2
Murrayfield Pl 1	49 E3
Murrayfield Rd	48 D2
Myrtle Ter	49 F5

N

Name	Ref
Napier Ln	49 G6
Napier Rd	49 G6
Nelson Pl 1	42 C1
Nelson St	42 C1
Nether Bakehouse 9	43 F2
Netherby Rd	45 H3
Nether Craigwell	43 F1
New Arthur Pl	43 E3
New Arthur St 5	43 E3
Newbattle Ter	50 A6
New Bells Ct 4	47 F3
New Broompark	45 F1
New Broughton	46 C6
New Cut Rigg	46 C3
Newhaven Main St	46 B1
Newhaven Pl	46 C1
Newhaven Rd	46 D4
Newington Rd	50 D5
New John's Pl	43 E4
Newkirkgate 2	47 E4
Newlands Pk	51 E6
New La	46 C2
New Orchardfield	47 E4
New Skinner's Cl	43 E2
News Steps	43 D2
New St	43 E2
Newton St	49 F5
Nichollfield	46 C2
Nicolson Sq	43 D3
Nicolson St	43 E3
Niddry St	43 E3
Niddry St S 3	43 E3
Nisbet Ct	47 G5
Noble Pl	47 G4
North Bk St	43 D2
North Br	43 D2
North Br Arc 10	43 D2
North Castle St	42 B1
North Charlotte St	42 B1
North Clyde St La 1	43 D1
Northcote St	49 G4
North E Circ Pl	42 B1
North Fort St	46 D2
North Hillhousefield	46 D2
North Junct St	46 D2
North Leith Mill 4	46 D2
North Leith Sands	46 D2
North Meadow Wk	42 C4
North Pk Ter	45 H6
North Richmond St 1	43 E3
North St. Andrew La	43 D1
North St. Andrew St	43 D1
North St. David St	43 D1
Northumberland Pl 2	42 C1
Northumberland Pl La	42 C1
Northumberland St	42 C1
Northumberland St N E La	42 C1
Northumberland St N W La	42 C1
Northumberland St S E La	42 C1
Northumberland St S W La	42 C1
Northview Ct	44 C3
North Werber Pk	45 F5
North Werber Pl	45 F4
North Werber Rd	45 F5
North W Circ Pl	42 B1
Norton Pk	47 F4
Nottingham Pl	43 E1

O

Name	Ref
Oakfield Pl	43 E3
Oakville Ter	47 G4
Ocean Dr	46 D2
Ocean Terminal Shop Cen	46 D1
Ogilvie Ter	49 F6
Old Assembly Cl 9	43 D2
Old Broughton 2	46 C6
Old Ch La	51 H4
Old Fishmarket Cl	43 D2
Old Tolbooth Wynd	43 E2
Orchard Bk	49 F1
Orchard Brae	45 G6
Orchard Brae Av	49 F1
Orchard Brae Gdns	49 F1
Orchard Brae Gdns W	49 F1
Orchard Brae W	45 G6
Orchard Cres	49 E1
Orchard Dr	49 E1
Orchardfield La	49 F1
Orchard Gro	45 G6
Orchard Pl	45 F6
Orchard Rd	49 F1
Orchard Rd S	49 E1
Orchard Ter	49 F1
Orchard Toll	49 F1
Ormidale Ter	48 D3
Orwell Pl	49 G4
Orwell Ter	49 G4
Osborne Ter	49 G3
Oxcars Ct	44 B3
Oxcraig St	45 G1
Oxford St	43 F4
Oxford Ter	42 A1

P

Name	Ref
Paisley Cres	51 H2
Paisley Gdns	51 H2
Paisley Ter	51 H2
Palmerston Pl	42 A2
Palmerston Pl La	42 A3
Palmerston Rd	50 C5
Panmure Pl	42 C4
Pape's Cotts	49 E3
Park Pl	46 B2
Park Rd	46 B2
Parkside St	43 F4
Parkside Ter	43 F4
Parkvale Pl	47 G4
Parliament Sq	43 D2
Parliament St	47 E3
Parsons Grn Ter 2	51 H1
Patrick Geddes Steps 14	42 C3
Patriothall 3	46 A6
Pattison St	47 F3
Peacock Ct	46 C1
Peel Ter	51 E6
Pembroke Pl	49 F3
Pennywell Cotts	44 C2
Pennywell Ct	44 C3
Pennywell Gdns	44 B3
Pennywell Gro	44 C3
Pennywell Medway	44 B3
Pennywell Pl	44 C3
Pennywell Rd	44 C3
Pennywell Vil	44 C2
Persevere Ct	47 E2
Perth St	46 A6
Picardy Pl	43 E1
Pier Pl	46 B1
Piershill La 3	51 H1
Piershill Pl 4	51 H1
Piershill Sq W	51 H1
Pilrig Cotts	47 E5
Pilrig Gdns	46 D4
Pilrig Glebe	47 E5
Pilrig Ho Cl	46 D4
Pilrig Ind Est	46 D4
Pilrig Pl	47 E5
Pilrig St	46 D4
Pilton Av	45 E3
Pilton Cres	45 G3
Pilton Dr	45 F3
Pilton Dr N	45 F3
Pilton Gdns	45 G3
Pilton Ln	45 F3
Pilton Pk	45 F3
Pilton Pl	45 F3
Pinkhill	48 A4
Pirniefield Bk	47 H4
Pirniefield Gdns	47 H4
Pirniefield Gro	47 H4
Pirniefield Pl	47 H4
Pirniefield Ter	47 H4
Pirrie St	47 E4
Pitlochry Pl	47 F6
Pitsligo Rd	50 A6
Pitt St	46 C3
Playfair Steps 1	42 C2
Pleasance	43 E3
Pollard Glebe	48 B6
Polwarth Cres	49 H5
Polwarth Gdns	49 G5
Polwarth Gro	49 G5
Polwarth Pk	49 G5
Polwarth Pl	49 G6
Polwarth Ter	49 G6
Ponton St	42 B4
Poplar La	47 F3
Porterfield Rd	45 F5

Portland Row 46 D2
Portland St 46 D2
Portland Ter 3 46 D2
Portsburgh Sq 5 42 C3
Potterrow 43 D3
Powderhall Brae 46 C4
Powderhall Rigg 46 C4
Powderhall Rd 46 C5
Prestonfield Av 51 F6
Prestonfield Bk 51 F6
Prestonfield Cres 51 F6
Prestonfield Gdns 51 F6
Prestonfield Rd 51 F6
Prestonfield Ter 51 F6
Priestfield Av 51 G6
Priestfield Cres 51 G6
Priestfield Gdns 51 G6
Priestfield Gro 51 F5
Priestfield Rd 51 F6
Priestfield Rd N 51 F5
Primrose Bk Rd 46 A2
Primrose St 47 F4
Primrose Ter 49 F5
Prince of Wales 47 E1
  Dock
Prince Regent St 46 D2
Princes Mall 43 D2
Princes St 42 C2
Prospect Bk Cres 47 G4
Prospect Bk Gdns 47 G5
Prospect Bk Gro 47 H4
Prospect Bk Pl 47 H4
Prospect Bk Rd 47 H4
Prospect Bk Ter 47 H4

Q

Quality St 44 A5
Quality St La 44 A5
Quarry Cl 43 E4
Quayside Mills 3 47 E3
Quayside St 47 E3
Queen Charlotte 47 F3
  La
Queen Charlotte 47 F3
  St
Queen's Av 44 C6
Queen's Av S 44 D6
Queen's Cres 51 E6
Queen's Dr 43 F3
Queensferry Rd 49 G1
Queensferry St 42 A2
Queensferry St La 42 A2
Queensferry Ter 49 F1
Queen's Gdns 44 D6
Queen's Pk Av 51 H2
Queen's Pk Ct 51 H2
Queen's Rd 44 D6
Queen St 42 C1
Queen St Gdns E 42 C1
Queen St Gdns W 42 C1
Quilts, The 46 D3
Quilts Wynd 46 D3

R

Raeburn Ms 45 H6
Raeburn Pl 45 H6
Raeburn St 45 H6
Ramsay Gdn 42 C2
Ramsay La 42 C2
Randolph Cliff 42 A2
Randolph Cres 42 A2
Randolph La 42 B2
Randolph Pl 42 B2
Rankeillor St 43 E4
Ratcliffe Ter 50 D5
Ravelston Ct 49 E2
Ravelston Dykes 49 E2
Ravelston Dykes 48 B2
  La
Ravelston Dykes 48 C1
  Rd
Ravelston Gdn 48 D2
Ravelston Hts 48 D1
Ravelston Ho Gro 48 D1
Ravelston Ho Ln 48 D1
Ravelston Ho Pk 48 D1

Ravelston Ho Rd 48 D1
Ravelston Pk 49 F2
Ravelston Pl 4 49 G2
Ravelston Ri 48 D2
Ravelston Ter 49 G1
Redbraes Gro 46 C4
Redbraes Pl 46 C4
Reekie's Ct 43 E3
Regent Br 2 43 D1
Regent Pl 51 F1
Regent Rd 43 E1
Regent's Ct 1 49 G4
Regent Ter 43 E1
Regent Ter Ms 43 F1
Register Pl 43 D1
Reid's Cl 43 F2
Reid's Ct 1 43 F2
Reid Ter 45 H6
Rennie's Isle 47 E2
Restalrig Av 51 H1
Restalrig Circ 47 H5
Restalrig Cres 47 H5
Restalrig Dr 47 H6
Restalrig Gdns 47 H6
Restalrig Pk 47 G5
Restalrig Rd 47 G4
Restalrig Rd S 51 H1
Restalrig Sq 47 H5
Restalrig Ter 47 F4
Richmond La 43 E3
Richmond Pl 43 E3
Richmond Ter 42 A3
Riego St 42 B3
Rillbank Cres 50 C5
Rillbank Ter 50 C5
Rintoul Pl 46 A6
Ritchie Pl 49 G5
Riversdale Cres 48 D4
Riversdale Gro 48 D3
Riversdale Rd 48 C3
Robb's Ln 48 D6
Robb's Ln Gro 48 D6
Robertson Av 49 E5
Robertson's Cl 43 E3
Robertson's Ct 2 43 F2
Rocheid Pk 45 G4
Rocheid Path 46 A5
Rochester Ter 49 H6
Rodney Pl 46 B6
Rodney St 46 B5
Romero Pl 51 E5
Ronaldson's Wf 47 E3
Rosebank Cotts 42 A3
Rosebank Gdns 45 H3
Rosebank Gro 45 H3
Rosebank Rd 45 H3
Rosebery Cres 49 G3
Rosebery Cres 49 G3
  La
Roseburn Av 49 E3
Roseburn Cliff 49 E3
Roseburn Cres 49 E4
Roseburn Dr 49 E3
Roseburn Gdns 2 49 E3
Roseburn 49 F3
  Maltings
Roseburn Pl 49 E3
Roseburn St 49 E4
Roseburn Ter 49 E3
Rosemount Bldgs 42 A3
Roseneath Pl 50 B5
Roseneath St 50 C5
Roseneath Ter 50 C5
Rose Pk 46 A3
Rose St 42 B2
Rose St N La 42 B2
Rose St S La 42 B2
Rosevale Pl 1 47 G4
Rosevale Ter 47 F4
Roseville Gdns 46 A2
Rossie Pl 47 E6
Rosslyn Cres 46 D5
Rosslyn Ter 46 D5
Rothesay Ms 49 G2
Rothesay Pl 49 G2
Rothesay Ter 49 G2

Roxburgh Pl 43 E3
Roxburgh St 43 E3
Royal Circ 42 B1
Royal Cres 46 B6
Royal Pk Pl 51 G1
Royal Pk Ter 51 G1
Royal Ter 43 E1
Royal Ter Ms 43 F1
Royston Mains 45 E2
  Av
Royston Mains 45 F2
  Cl
Royston Mains 45 E2
  Cres
Royston Mains 45 F2
  Gdns
Royston Mains 45 F2
  Grn
Royston Mains 45 E2
  Pl
Royston Mains 45 F2
  Rd
Royston Mains 45 E2
  St
Royston Ter 46 A4
Russell Gdns 49 F3
Russell Pl 46 A2
Russell Rd 49 F3
Rutland Ct 2 42 B3
Rutland Ct La 42 B3
Rutland Pl 1 42 B2
Rutland Sq 42 B2
Rutland St 42 B2
Ryehill Av 47 G4
Ryehill Gdns 47 G4
Ryehill Gro 47 G5
Ryehill Pl 47 G4
Ryehill Ter 47 G4

S

St. Andrew Pl 47 F4
St. Andrew Sq 43 D1
St. Anthony La 47 E3
St. Anthony Pl 5 47 E3
St. Anthony St 6 47 E3
St. Bernard's Cres 42 A1
St. Bernard's Row 46 A6
St. Catherine's 48 B4
  Gdns
St. Catherine's Pl 50 D5
St. Clair Av 47 F5
St. Clair Pl 47 F5
St. Clair Rd 47 F5
St. Clair St 47 F5
St. Colme St 42 B2
St. David's Pl 9 42 A3
St. David's Ter 10 42 A3
St. Giles' St 43 D2
St. James Cen 43 D1
St. James' Pl 43 D1
St. James Sq 43 D1
St. John's Cres 48 A4
St. John's Hill 9 43 E2
St. John St 43 E2
St. Leonard's Bk 43 F4
St. Leonard's 43 F4
  Crag 1
St. Leonard's Hill 43 E4
St. Leonard's La 43 F4
St. Leonard's St 43 E4
St. Margaret's Pl 50 B6
St. Margaret's Rd 50 A6
St. Mary's St 43 E2
St. Ninian's Row 3 43 D1
St. Patrick Sq 43 E4
St. Patrick St 3 43 E4
St. Peter's Bldgs 42 A4
St. Peter's Pl 42 A4
St. Stephen Pl 46 A6
St. Stephen St 46 A6
St. Teresa Pl 49 G6
St. Thomas Rd 50 D5
St. Vincent St 46 B6
Salamander Pl 47 G3
Salamander St 47 F3
Salamander Yards 47 H4

Salisbury Ms 51 E5
Salisbury Pl 50 D5
Salisbury Rd 51 E5
Salmond Pl 47 F6
Salvesen Cres 44 B2
Salvesen Gdns 44 C2
Salvesen Gro 44 C2
Salvesen Ter 44 C2
Sand Port 47 F2
Sandport Pl 47 E2
Sandport St 47 E2
Sandport Way 47 E3
Sauchiebank 49 F4
Saughton Av 48 D5
Saughton Cres 48 C4
Saughton Gdns 48 C4
Saughton Gro 48 C4
Saughtonhall Av 48 C4
Saughtonhall Av 48 C4
  W
Saughtonhall 48 D4
  Circ
Saughtonhall 48 C4
  Cres
Saughtonhall Dr 48 C3
Saughtonhall 48 D4
  Gdns
Saughtonhall Gro 48 D4
Saughtonhall Pl 48 D4
Saughtonhall Ter 48 D4
Saughton Ln 48 C4
Saughton Mains 48 A6
  Av
Saughton Mains 48 A6
  Bk
Saughton Mains 48 A6
  Pk
Saughton Mains 48 A6
  St
Saughton Mains 48 A6
  Ter
Saughton Pk 48 C4
Saughton Rd 48 C4
Saunders St 42 B1
Saxe-Coburg Pl 46 A6
Saxe-Coburg St 46 A6
Saxe-Coburg Ter 4 46 A6
Sciennes 50 D5
Sciennes Gdns 50 D5
Sciennes Hill Pl 50 D5
Sciennes Ho Pl 50 D5
Sciennes Pl 2 50 D5
Sciennes Rd 50 C5
Scone Gdns 51 H1
Scotland St 46 B6
Seacot 1 47 H4
Seafield Av 47 H4
Seafield Pl 47 H4
Seafield Rd 47 H4
Seaforth Dr 44 D6
Seaforth Ter 44 D6
Sealcarr St 45 F1
Seaport St 5 47 F3
Semple St 42 B3
Seton Pl 50 D5
Shaftesbury Pk 49 F6
Shandon Cres 49 F6
Shandon Pl 49 F6
Shandon Rd 49 F6
Shandon St 49 F6
Shandon Ter 49 F6
Shandwick Pl 42 A3
Shaw's Pl 46 D5
Shaw's Sq 2 46 D6
Shaw's St 46 D5
Shaw's Ter 46 D5
Sheriff Bk 47 E3
Sheriff Brae 47 E3
Sheriff Pk 47 E3
Shore 47 F3
Shore Pl 47 F3
Shrub Pl 46 D5
Shrub Pl La 46 D5
Sienna Gdns 50 D5
Silverknowes Bk 44 A4
Silverknowes Brae 44 A4

Silverknowes Ct 44 A4
Silverknowes Cres 44 A3
Silverknowes Dell 44 B4
Silverknowes Dr 44 A4
Silverknowes 44 A4
  Eastway
Silverknowes 44 A3
  Gdns
Silverknowes Grn 44 B4
Silverknowes Gro 44 A3
Silverknowes Hill 44 A4
Silverknowes 44 B4
  Midway
Silverknowes 44 B5
  Neuk
Silverknowes 44 A3
  Parkway
Silverknowes Pl 44 A3
Silverknowes Rd 44 A3
Silverknowes Rd E 44 A4
Silverknowes Rd S 44 A5
Silverknowes 44 B4
  Southway
Silverknowes Vw 44 B4
Silvermills 46 A6
Simon Sq 4 43 E3
Sinclair Cl 2 49 F6
Sinclair Gdns 49 F5
Sinclair Pl 49 E6
Slateford Rd 49 E6
Slateford Rd Br 49 F6
Slater's Steps 6 43 F2
Sleigh Dr 47 G6
Sleigh Gdns 47 H6
Sloan St 47 E5
Smithfield St 49 E5
Smith's Pl 47 E4
Solicitor's Bldgs 4 43 D7
Somerset Pl 47 F4
South Beechwood 48 B4
South Br 43 D2
South Charlotte St 42 B2
South Clerk St 43 E4
South Coll St 43 D2
South E Circ Pl 1 42 B1
South Ettrick Rd 49 G6
South Fort St 46 D3
South Gayfield 46 D6
  La
South Gillsland 49 G6
  Rd
South Gray's Cl 43 E2
South Gray St 51 E6
South Groathill Av 44 D6
South Lauder Rd 50 D6
South 46 B2
  Laverockbank Av
South 49 G1
  Learmonth Av
South 49 G1
  Learmonth Gdns
South Lorne Pl 47 E5
South Meadow 42 C4
  Wk
South Oxford St 51 E5
South Pk 46 C2
South St. Andrew 43 D1
  St
South St. David St 43 D1
South Sloan St 47 E5
South Trinity Rd 46 A3
Spencer Pl 46 A2
Spence St 51 E5
Spey St 46 D5
Spey St La 46 D5
Spey Ter 46 D5
Spier's Pl 7 47 E3
Spittalfield Cres 43 E4
Spittal St 42 B3
Spittal St La 3 42 B3
Spottiswoode Rd 50 B5
Spottiswoode St 50 B5
Springfield 46 D4
Springfield 47 E4
  Bldgs 3
Springfield La 47 E4

Springfield St 47 E4
Spring Gdns 51 F1
Springwell Pl 49 G4
Spylaw Rd 49 G6
Stafford St 42 A2
Stair Pk 48 D3
Stanhope Pl 49 F3
Stanhope St 49 F3
Stanley Pl 51 F1
Stanley Rd 46 B2
Stanwell St 47 E4
Starbank Rd 46 B2
Stead's Pl 47 E4
Stenhouse Av 48 B5
Stenhouse Av W 48 B6
Stenhouse Cres 48 B6
Stenhouse Cross 48 B6
Stenhouse Dr 48 B6
Stenhouse Gdns 48 B6
Stenhouse Gdns 48 B6
N
Stenhouse Gro 48 B6
Stenhouse Pl E 48 B6
Stenhouse Pl W 48 B6
Stenhouse St E 48 B6
Stenhouse St W 48 A6
Stenhouse Ter 48 C6
Stevenlaw's Cl 43 D2
Stevenson Av 48 D5
Stevenson Dr 48 B6
Stevenson Gro 48 D5
Stevenson Rd 48 D5
Stevenson Ter 48 D5
Stewartfield 46 C4
Stewart Ter 49 E5
Stirling Rd 46 A2
Strachan Gdns 44 B6
Strachan Rd 48 C1
Stratearn Pl 50 A6
Stratearn Rd 50 B6
Succoth Av 49 E2
Succoth Ct 49 E2
Succoth Gdns 49 E2
Succoth Pk 48 D2
Succoth Pl 49 E2
Summerbank 46 B6
Summerfield 47 G4
Gdns
Summerfield Pl 47 G4
Summerhall 4 50 D5
Summerhall 43 E4
Cres 4
Summerhall Pl 5 50 D5
Summerhall Sq 50 D5
Summer Pl 46 B5
Summerside Pl 46 C3
Summerside St 46 C3
Sunbury Ms 49 G2
Sunbury Pl 49 G2
Sunbury St 49 G2
Sunnybank 51 G1
Sunnybank Pl 51 G1
Sunnybank Ter 4 51 F1
Sunnyside 47 F6
Surrey Pl 2 49 F3
Sutherland St 49 F3
Swanfield 47 E3
Sylvan Pl 50 C5

T
Tanfield 46 B5
Tantallon Pl 50 D5
Tarvit St 42 B4
Taylor Gdns 47 E3
Taylor Pl 51 F1
Tay St 49 G5
Telfer Sub 49 G4
Telford Dr 45 E5
Telford Gdns 45 E5
Telford Pl 45 E5
Telford Rd 45 E6
Temple Pk Cres 49 G5
Tennant St 47 E4
Terrars Cft 43 F4
Teviotdale Pl 46 A6
Teviot Pl 43 D3

Thirlestane La 50 B6
Thirlestane Rd 50 B5
Thistle Ct 3 42 C1
Thistle Pl 42 A4
Thistle St 42 C1
Thistle St N E La 42 C1
Thistle St N W La 42 C1
Thistle St S E La 42 C1
Thistle St S W La 42 C1
Thomson's Ct 8 42 C3
Thorntreeside 47 F4
Thorntree St 47 E4
Thornville Ter 47 F5
Thornybauk 42 B3
Timber Bush 47 F2
Tinto Pl 46 D4
Tipperlinn Rd 49 H6
Tolbooth Wynd 47 F3
Torphichen Pl 42 A3
Torphichen St 42 A3
Tower Pl 47 F2
Tower St 47 F2
Tower St La 47 F2
Townswomen's 43 D4
Guild Wk
Trafalgar La 46 C3
Trafalgar St 46 D3
Traquair Pk E 48 A4
Trinity Ct 46 A3
Trinity Cres 46 A1
Trinity Gro 46 A2
Trinity Mains 46 A3
Trinity Rd 46 A2
Trinity Way 46 A3
Tron Sq 12 43 D2
Tynecastle La 49 F5
Tynecastle Ter 49 F5
Tytler Ct 51 F1
Tytler Gdns 43 F1

U
Ulster Cres 51 H2
Ulster Dr 51 H2
Union Pl 2 43 E1
Union St 46 C6
Upper Bow 8 43 D2
Upper Coltbridge 49 E2
Ter
Upper Damside 49 G2
Upper Dean Ter 42 A1
Upper Gilmore Pl 42 B4
Upper Gilmore Ter 42 B4
Upper Gray St 50 D5
Upper Greenside 43 E1
La 7
Upper Gro Pl 42 A4
Upper Hermitage 47 F4

V
Valleyfield St 42 B4
Vanburgh Pl 47 F4
Veitch's Sq 46 A6
Vennel 42 C3
Ventnor Pl 51 F6
Ventnor Ter 51 E6
Victoria Dock 47 E2
Victoria St 43 D3
Victoria Ter 9 42 C3
Viewcraig Gdns 43 E2
Viewcraig St 43 E2
Viewforth 42 A4
Viewforth Gdns 50 A5
Viewforth Sq 49 H5
Viewforth Ter 49 H5
Violet Ter 49 F5
Vivian Ter 44 A5

W
Walker St 42 A2
Walker Ter 6 42 A3
Warden's Cl 43 D3
Wardie Av 45 H3
Wardieburn Dr 45 G2
Wardieburn Pl E 45 G2
Wardieburn Pl N 45 G2
Wardieburn Pl S 45 G2

Wardieburn Pl W 45 F2
Wardieburn Rd 45 F2
Wardieburn St E 45 G2
Wardieburn St W 45 F2
Wardieburn Ter 45 F2
Wardie Cres 45 G2
Wardie Dell 45 H2
Wardiefield 45 G2
Wardie Gro 45 G2
Wardie Ho La 45 H1
Wardie Pk 45 H3
Wardie Rd 45 H3
Wardie Sq 45 H2
Wardie Steps 45 H2
Wardlaw Pl 49 F5
Wardlaw St 49 F5
Wardlaw Ter 49 F5
Warrender Pk 50 A5
Cres
Warrender Pk 50 B5
Rd
Warrender Pk 50 B5
Ter
Warriston Av 46 B4
Warriston Cres 46 B5
Warriston Dr 46 A4
Warriston Gdns 46 A4
Warriston Gro 46 A4
Warriston Pl 46 B5
Warriston Rd 46 B3
Warriston Ter 46 A4
Washington La 49 G4
Washington St 49 G4
Waterloo Pl 43 D1
Water's Cl 6 47 F3
Water St 47 F3
Watson Cres 49 G5
Waverley Br 43 D2
Waverley Pk 51 F1
Waverley Pk Ter 51 F1
Waverley Pl 51 F1
Waverley St 43 D2
Websters Land 10 42 C3
Well Ct 4 42 A2
Wellington Pl 47 F3
Wellington St 47 E6
Wemyss Pl 42 B1
Wemyss Pl Ms 42 B1
Werberside Ms 45 F4
West Adam St 43 E3
West Annandale 46 C5
St
West App Rd 42 B3
West Bow 43 D3
West Bowl Grn St 46 D3
West Bryson Rd 49 G5
West Castle Rd 49 H5
West Catherine Pl 49 F3
West Cherrybank 46 B2
West Coates 49 F3
West Coll St 43 D3
West Ct 48 D1
West Cromwell 47 E2
St 1
West 43 E4
Crosscauseway
West End 42 B2
West End Pl 49 G4
Wester Cl 3 46 C1
Wester Coates Av 49 F3
Wester Coates 49 F3
Gdns
Wester Coates Pl 49 F2
Wester Coates Rd 49 F3
Wester Coates Ter 49 F3
Wester Drylaw Av 44 C5
Wester Drylaw Dr 44 C5
Wester Drylaw Pk 44 D5
Wester Drylaw Pl 44 C5
Wester Drylaw 44 D6
Row
Western Cor 1 48 D3
Western Gdns 48 D3
Western Harbour 46 D1
Western Pl 48 D3
Western Ter 48 D3

West Ferryfield 45 G3
Westfield Av 48 D5
Westfield Ct 48 D5
Westfield Rd 49 E5
Westfield St 49 E5
West Fountain Pl 49 G4
West Gorgie Pk 48 D6
West Gra Gdns 50 C6
West Granton 45 E2
Access
West Granton Rd 45 F2
Westhall Gdns 50 A5
West Harbour Rd 50 C6
West Maitland St 42 A3
West Mayfield 51 E6
West Mill La 42 A2
West Montgomery 46 D6
Pl
West Newington 50 D5
Pl
West Nicolson St 43 E3
West Norton Pl 43 F1
West Pk Pl 49 G4
West Pier 45 F1
West Pilton Av 44 D4
West Pilton Bk 44 C3
West Pilton Cres 44 C3
West Pilton 44 D3
Crossway
West Pilton Dr 44 D3
West Pilton Gdns 44 D3
West Pilton Grn 44 D3
West Pilton Gro 44 D4
West Pilton Lea 44 D3
West Pilton Ln 44 D3
West Pilton March 45 E2
West Pilton Pk 44 D3
West Pilton Pl 45 E3
West Pilton Ri 44 D3
West Pilton Rd 45 E3
West Pilton St 44 D3
West Pilton Ter 44 D3
West Pilton Vw 44 D4
West Port 42 C3
West Preston St 50 D5
West Register St 43 D1
West Register St 43 D1
La 4
West Richmond St 43 E3
West Scotland St 46 B6
La
West Shore Rd 44 C2
West Shore Rd 44 D1
Trd Est
West Silvermills 46 A6
La
West Stanhope 49 F3
Pl 1
West Tollcross 42 B4
West Werberside 45 F4
West Winnelstrae 45 G4
West Wds 45 F5
Wheatfield Pl 49 E5
Wheatfield Rd 49 E5
Wheatfield St 49 F5
Wheatfield Ter 1 49 E5
Whitehall Ct 44 C6
White Horse Cl 43 F2
Whitehouse Ln 50 A5
Whitehouse Ter 50 B6
White Pk 49 F5
Whitingford 46 C3
Whitson Cres 48 C5
Whitson Gro 48 C5
Whitson Pl E 48 C5
Whitson Pl W 48 C5
Whitson Rd 48 C5
Whitson Ter 48 C5
Whitson Wk 48 B5
Whitson Way 48 C5
Whyte Pl 51 F1
Wilfrid Ter 5 51 H1
William St 42 A2
William St La N E 42 A2
William St La N W 42 A2
William St La S E 42 A2

William St La S W 42 A3
Willowbank Row 46 C2
Willowbrae Av 51 H2
Willowbrae Rd 51 H2
Wilson's Ct 3 43 E2
Windmill La 43 D4
Windmill Pl 6 43 E4
Windmill St 43 D4
Windsor St 46 D6
Windsor St La 46 D6
Wishaw Ter 51 G1
Wolseley Cres 51 H1
Wolseley Gdns 8 51 H1
Wolseley Pl 9 51 H1
Wolseley Ter 6 51 H1
Woodbine Ter 47 F5
Woodville Ter 47 F5
Wright's Hos 50 A5
Wyvern Pk 50 C6

Y
Yardheads 47 E3
Yeaman La 49 G4
Yeaman Pl 49 G4
York Bldgs 7 43 D1
York La 43 D1
York Pl 43 D1
York Rd 46 B2
Young St 42 B2
Young St La N 42 B2
Young St La S 42 B2

Z
Zetland Pl 46 A2

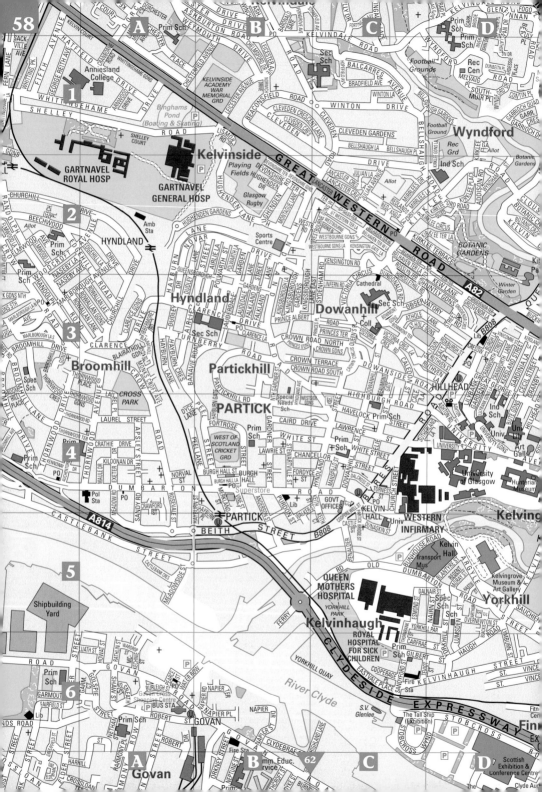

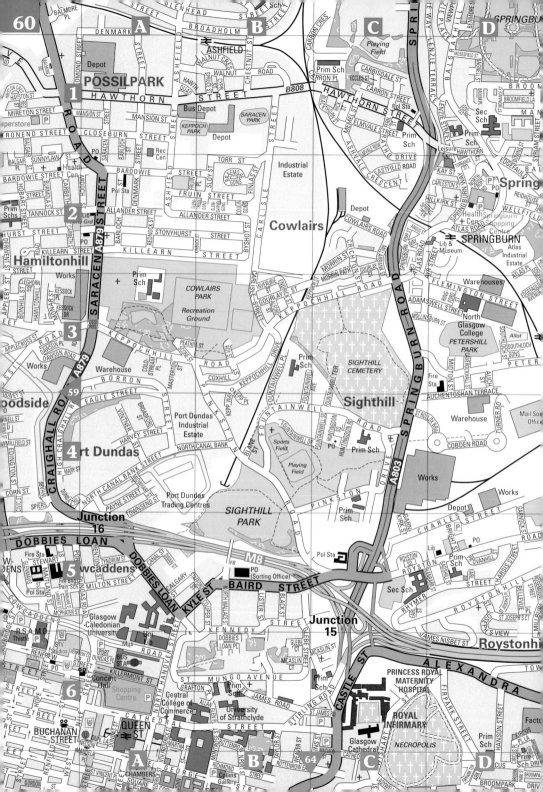

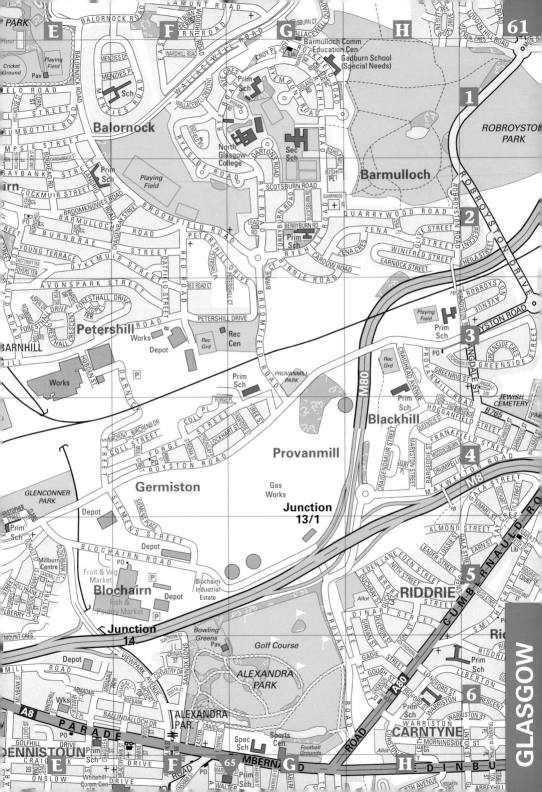

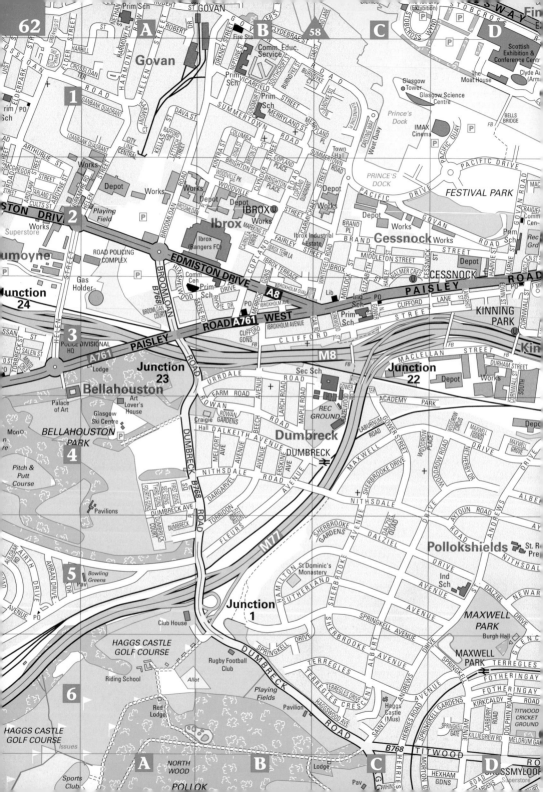

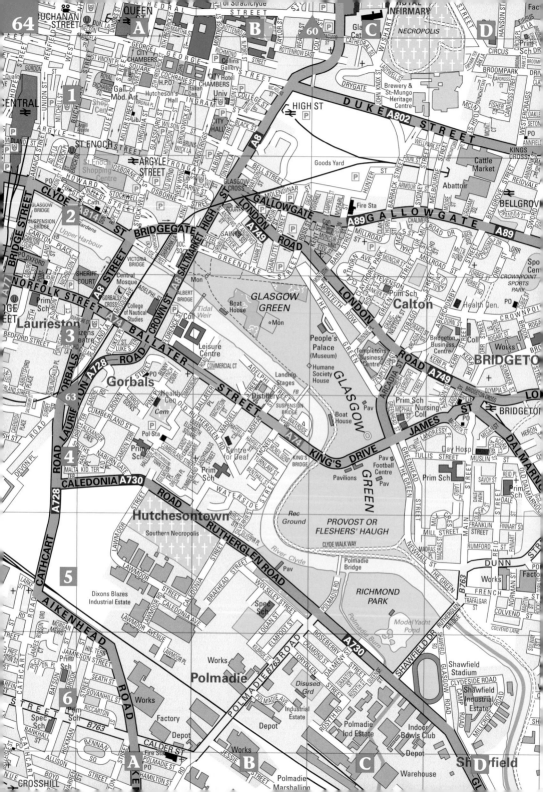

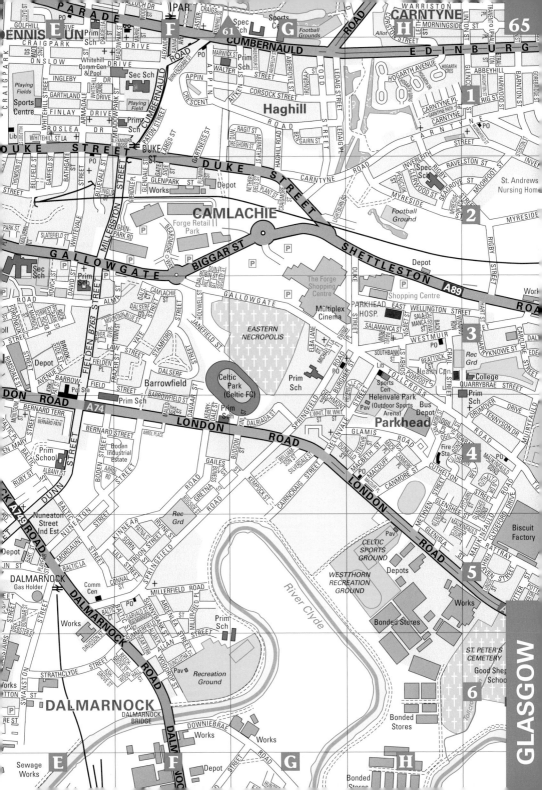

This index contains streets that are not named on the map due to insufficient space. For each of these cases the nearest street that does appear on the map is shown in *italics*.

A

Abbotsford Pl	63 H3
Abercromby Dr	64 D2
Abercromby Sq	64 D2
Abercromby St	64 D3
Aberdour St	65 G1
Aberfeldy St	65 G1
Aberfoyle St	65 G1
Abernethy St	65 G1
Academy Pk	64 D4
Acorn Ct	64 D4
Acorn St	64 D4
Adams Ct La	63 H2
Adamswell St	60 C3
Addison Rd	58 D2
Adelphi St	64 B3
Admiral St	63 E3
Aikenhead Rd	63 H5
Aird's La	64 A2
Bridgegate	
Airlie La	58 B2
Airlie St	58 A3
Aitken St	65 G1
Albany St	65 E4
Albert Br	64 A3
Albert Cross	63 F5
Albert Dr	62 C6
Albion Gate	64 B1
Albion St	
Albion St	64 B2
Alexander Cres	64 A4
Alexandra Ct	61 F6
Alexandra Cross	65 F1
Alexandra Par	60 C6
Alexandra Pk St	65 F1
Alford St	60 B3
Alfred La	58 D3
Alfred Ter	59 E3
Allander St	60 A2
Allan Glen Pl	60 B6
Allan Pl	65 F5
Allan St	65 F6
Allison Pl	63 G6
Prince Edward St	
Allison St	63 G6
Alma St	65 E3
Almond St	61 H5
Alston La	64 C2
Claythorn St	
Amisfield St	59 E1
Anchor La	64 A1
St. Vincent Pl	
Ancroft St	59 G3
Anderson St	58 B4
Anderston Cross	63 G1
Cen	
Anderston Quay	63 F2
Angus St	60 C2
Annandale St	63 H5
Annbank Pl	64 D2
Annbank St	64 D2
Annette St	63 G6
Annfield Pl	64 D1
Anson St	64 D4
Anthony St	63 G1
Appin Cres	65 F1
Appin Rd	65 F1
Appleby St	59 H3
Applecross St	59 H3
Apsley La	58 A4
Apsley St	
Apsley St	58 A4
Arcadia Pl	64 C3
Arcadia St	64 C3
Ardbeg La	63 G6
Ardbeg St	63 G6
Ardenlea St	65 F5
Ardery St	58 A4
Apsley St	
Ardessie Pl	58 D1
Ardoch St	60 A2
Ardo Gdns	62 A3
Hinshelwood Dr	

Argyle St	63 G1
Argyll Arc	64 A1
Ark La	64 D1
Arlington St	59 F5
Armadale Ct	61 E6
Armadale Path	61 E6
Armadale Pl	61 E6
Armadale St	65 E1
Armour St	64 C2
Arnwood Dr	58 A1
Arrol Pl	65 F4
Arrol Rd	65 E4
Arthur St	58 D5
Ascog St	63 G6
Ashfield St	60 A2
Ashgrove St	65 E6
Ashley La	59 F5
Ashley St	59 F5
Ashton La	58 D4
Ashton La N	58 D4
Ashton La	
Ashton Rd	58 D4
Ashvale Cres	60 C1
Aspen Dr	61 E3
Athole Gdns	58 C3
Athole La	58 C3
Atlas Ind Est	60 D2
Atlas Pl	60 D3
Atlas Rd	60 C2
Atlas Sq	60 D2
Ayr St	
Auchentoshan	60 D4
Ter	
Auchinloch St	60 D3
Auckland St	59 H3
Avenuepark St	59 E2
Avenue St	61 E3
Avonspark St	61 E3
Ayr St	60 C3
Aytoun Rd	62 D5

B

Back Causeway	65 H3
Bagnall St	60 D1
Bain Sq	64 C2
Bain St	
Bain St	64 C2
Bairds Brae	59 H3
Baird St	60 B5
Balaclava St	63 G1
McAlpine St	
Balcarres Av	58 C1
Balgair Pl	59 H2
Balgair St	59 H1
Balglass Gdns	59 H2
Balglass St	59 H2
Balgraybank St	60 D2
Balgrayhill Rd	60 D1
Baliol La	59 F5
Baliol St	59 F5
Ballater Pl	64 B4
Ballater St	64 A3
Ballindalloch Dr	61 E6
Ballindarroch La	61 E6
Armadale St	
Balmore Sq	59 H1
Balornock Rd	61 E1
Baltic Ct	65 E5
Baltic St	
Baltic La	65 E5
Baltic Pl	65 E4
Baltic St	65 E4
Banavie La	58 B3
Banavie Rd	
Banavie Rd	58 A3
Bankhall St	63 H6
Bankier St	64 C3
Bank St	59 E4
Bannatyne Av	65 F1
Barbreck Rd	63 G6
Pollokshaws Rd	
Barclay St	60 D1
Lenzie St	

Bardowie St	59 H2
Bargeddie St	61 H4
Barloch St	60 A2
Barmulloch Rd	61 E2
Barnhill Dr	61 E3
Foresthall Dr	
Barrack St	64 C2
Barrington Dr	59 F4
Barrland St	63 G5
Barrowfield St	65 E3
Barr St	59 G3
Bartholomew St	65 E5
Bathgate St	65 E2
Bath La	59 G6
Bath La W	59 F6
North St	
Bath St	59 G6
Batson St	63 H6
Beaconsfield Rd	58 B1
Beardmore Way	65 F2
Beaton Rd	63 E6
Beattock St	65 H3
Beaumont Gate	58 C3
Bedford La	63 H3
Bedford St	63 H3
Beech Av	62 B3
Beechgrove St	65 F6
Beith St	58 B5
Belgrave La	59 E3
Belgrave Ter	59 E3
Belhaven Cres La	58 C2
Kensington Rd	
Belhaven Ter	58 C2
Belhaven Ter La	58 C2
Belhaven Ter W	58 C2
Belhaven Ter W La	58 C2
Bellevue Pl	60 D5
Bellfield St	65 E2
Bellgrove St	64 D2
Bellshaugh Gdns	58 C1
Bellshaugh La	58 C1
Bellshaugh Pl	58 C1
Bellshaugh Rd	58 C1
Bell St	64 B2
Belmont Cres	59 E3
Belmont La	59 E3
Belmont St	59 E3
Beltane St	59 F6
Benalder St	58 C5
Bengairn St	65 G1
Bennan Sq	64 A6
Benny Lynch Ct	64 A3
Benthall St	64 B4
Bentinck St	59 E5
Benview St	59 F2
Berkeley St	59 E5
Berkeley Ter La	59 F6
Elderslie St	
Bernard Path	65 E4
Bernard St	65 E4
Bernard Ter	65 E4
Berryburn Rd	61 G2
Biggar St	65 F2
Bilsland Ct	59 H1
Bilsland Dr	59 F1
Binnie Pl	64 C3
Birchend Dr	61 F4
Birchend Pl	61 F4
Birch St	64 B5
Birkenshaw St	65 F1
Birkwood St	65 F6
Dalmarnock Rd	
Birnam Rd	65 H5
Birnie Ct	61 G3
Birnie Rd	61 G2
Bishopmill Pl	61 G1
Bishopmill Rd	61 G1
Bishop St	63 G1
Blackburn St	62 D2

Blackfriars St	64 B1
Blackie St	58 D6
Black St	60 B5
Blackthorn St	60 C1
Blairathol Av	58 A3
Blairatholl Gdns	58 A3
Blane St	60 B4
Blantyre St	58 D5
Blochairn Rd	61 E5
Bluevale St	65 E2
Blythswood Ct	63 G1
Cadogan St	
Blythswood Sq	59 G6
Blythswood St	63 G1
Boden Ind Est	65 F4
Boden St	65 E4
Boghead Rd	61 E1
Bogside St	65 F4
Boleyn Rd	63 E6
Bonawe St	59 F2
Kirkland St	
Boness St	65 F4
Bonhill St	59 H3
Bonnar St	65 E5
Borron St	60 A3
Botanic Cres	58 D2
Botanic Cres La	58 D2
Bothwell La	63 G1
Blythswood St	
Bothwell St	59 G6
Boundary Rd	64 C6
Rutherglen Rd	
Bower St	59 E3
Bowman St	63 G6
Bowmont Gdns	58 C3
Bowmont Ter	58 C3
Bradford Av	58 C1
Braehead St	64 B5
Braemore Gdns	60 B2
Braeside St	59 F3
Braid Sq	59 G4
Braid St	59 G4
Brandon St	64 D2
Brand Pl	62 C2
Brand St	62 C2
Breadalbane St	59 F6
St. Vincent St	
Brechin St	59 E6
Bridgegate	
Bridgegate Path	64 A2
Bridgegate	
Bridge St	63 H2
Bridgeton	64 D3
Business Cen	
Bridgeton Cross	64 D3
Brighton Pl	62 B2
Brighton St	62 B2
Bright St	60 D5
Briton St	62 B2
Broadford St	60 A4
Broad St	64 D3
Brodick St	61 E3
Brookside St	65 E3
Brook St	64 D3
Broomfield La	60 D1
Broomfield Rd	60 D1
Broomielaw	63 G2
Broomknowes Rd	61 E2
Broomloan Ct	62 A3
Broomloan Pl	62 A2
Broomloan Rd	62 A2
Broompark Circ	60 D6
Broompark Dr	64 D1
Broompark La	64 D1
Broompark St	64 D1
Brora La	61 H5
Brora St	
Brora St	61 H5
Brown St	63 G1
Bruce Rd	63 E4
Brunswick La	64 A1

Brunswick St	64 A1
Buccleuch La	59 G5
Rose St	
Buccleuch St	59 G5
Buchanan St	63 H1
Buchan St	63 H3
Norfolk St	
Buckingham St	58 D3
Buckingham Ter	58 D3
Bucksburn Rd	61 G2
Buddon St	65 G4
Bunhouse Rd	58 C5
Burgher St	65 G3
Burgh Hall La	58 B4
Burgh Hall St	58 B4
Burgh La	58 D3
Burleigh St	58 A6
Burmola St	59 H2
Burnbank Gdns	59 F4
Burnbank La	59 F4
Napiershall St	
Burnbank Pl	59 G4
(Woodside)	
Burnbank Ter	
Burnbank Pl	64 C1
Drygate	
Burnbank Ter	59 F4
Burnbrae St	61 E2
Burndyke Ct	62 B1
Burndyke Sq	62 C1
Burndyke St	62 B1
Burns St	59 H4
Burrells La	64 C1
Bute Gdns	58 D4
Bute La	58 D4
Great George St	
Butterbiggins Rd	63 G5
Butterfield Pl	63 G5
Pollokshaws Rd	
Byres Rd	58 C4
Byshot St	60 B2

C

Cadogan St	63 G1
Cadzow St	63 G1
Caird Dr	58 B4
Cairncraig St	65 G4
Cairnlea Dr	62 B2
Caithness St	59 F2
Caldarvan St	59 H3
Calder St	63 H6
Caledonia Av	64 A5
Caledonian Cres	59 E4
Great Western Rd	
Caledonia Rd	63 H4
Caledonia St	64 A5
Caledon La	58 C3
Caledon St	58 C3
Calgary St	60 A5
Callander St	59 G3
Calton Entry	64 C2
Gallowgate	
Cambridge St	59 H6
Camden Ter	64 A4
Camlachie St	65 F3
Camp Rd	64 D6
Campsie St	60 D1
Canal St	60 A5
Candleriggs	64 B2
Canmore Pl	65 H4
Canmore St	65 H4
Canting Way	62 C1
Carberry Rd	62 D6
Carbeth St	59 H2
Carbisdale St	60 D1
Carbrook St	61 E5
Cardarrach St	61 E1
Cardow Rd	61 H5
Cardross Ct	64 D1
Cardross St	64 D1
Cardwell St	63 G4
Eglinton St	
Cardyke St	61 E2

Carfin St 63 H6
Carfrae St 58 C6
Carillon Rd 62 C2
Carleston St 60 D2
Carlisle St 60 B2
Carlton Ct 63 H2
Carlton Pl 63 H2
Carmichael St 62 B2
Carnarvon St 59 F5
Carnoustie Pl 63 F3
Carnoustie St 63 F3
Carntyne Path 65 H1
Carntyne Pl 65 H1
Carntyne Rd 65 G2
Carrick St 63 G2
Carrington St 59 F4
Carron Cres 60 B1
Carron Pl 60 B1
Carron St 60 C1
Carstairs St 65 E6
Castlebank Cres 58 A5
Castle Cres N Ct 64 A1
 Royal Ex Sq
Castle St 60 C6
Castle St 58 C5
 (Partick)
Cathedral Sq 64 C1
Cathedral St 60 A6
Catherine Pl 63 F1
 Hydepark St
Cavendish Ct 63 H4
Cavendish Pl 63 H4
Cavendish St 63 H4
Cecil St 58 D3
Cedar Ct 59 G4
Cedar St 59 G4
Central Sta 63 H1
Centre St 63 G3
Cessnock St 62 C2
Chalmers Ct 64 C2
Chalmers Gate 64 C2
 Claythorn St
Chalmers Pl 64 C2
 Claythorn St
Chalmers St 64 C2
Chancellor St 58 B4
Chapel St 59 E1
Chapman St 63 G6
 Allison St
Charing Cross 59 F5
Charing Cross La 59 F6
 Granville St
Charles St 60 C5
Charlotte La 64 B2
 London Rd
Charlotte La S 64 B2
 Charlotte St
Charlotte La W 64 B2
 London Rd
Charlotte St 64 B2
Cheapside St 63 F2
Chelmsford Dr 58 B1
Chesterfield Av 58 A1
Chestnut St 60 B1
Chisholm St 64 B2
Christopher St 61 E4
Churchill Dr 58 A3
Church St 58 C4
Circus Dr 64 D1
Circus Pl 64 D1
Circus Pl La 60 D6
City Link Cen 62 A1
Civic St 59 H4
Clairmont Gdns 59 F5
Claremont Pas 59 F5
 Claremont Ter
Claremont Pl 59 F5
 Claremont Ter
Claremont St 59 E6
Claremont Ter 59 F5
Claremont Ter 59 E5
 La
Clarence Dr 58 A3
Clarence Gdns 58 A3
Clarence La 58 B3

Clarendon La 59 G4
 Clarendon St
Clarendon Pl 59 G4
Clarendon St 59 G4
Clare St 61 E4
Clayslaps Rd 58 D5
Claythorn Av 64 C3
Claythorn Circ 64 C2
 Claythorn Av
Claythorn Ct 64 C2
 Claythorn Pk
Claythorn Pk 64 C3
Claythorn St 64 C2
Claythorn Ter 64 C2
 Claythorn Pk
Clayton Ter 64 D1
Cleghorn St 59 H3
Cleland La 64 A3
Cleland St 64 A3
Clerwood St 65 H2
Cleveden Cres 58 B1
Cleveden Cres La 58 B1
Cleveden Dr 58 B1
Cleveden Dr La 58 C2
 Mirrlees Dr
Cleveden Gdns 58 C1
Cleveland La 59 F6
 Kent Rd
Cleveland St 59 F6
Clifford Gdns 62 B3
Clifford La 62 C3
Clifford Pl 62 D2
 Clifford St
Clifford St 62 B3
Cliff Rd 59 F5
Clifton Pl 59 E5
 Clifton St
Clifton St 59 E5
Closeburn St 60 A1
Clouston Ct 59 E2
 Fergus Dr
Clouston La 59 E2
Clouston St 58 D2
Cloverbank St 61 E5
Clutha St 62 D2
 Paisley Rd W
Clydebrae St 58 B6
Clyde Ind Cen 59 E6
Clyde Pl 63 G2
Clydeside 58 C6
 Expressway
Clydeside Rd 64 D6
Clyde St 63 H2
Clynder St 62 B2
Coalhill St 65 F3
Cobden Rd 60 D4
Coburg St 63 H3
Cochrane St 64 A1
Cockmuir St 61 E2
Colbert St 64 D5
Coldstream Pl 60 A3
Colebrooke La 59 E3
 Colebrooke St
Colebrooke Pl 59 E3
Colebrooke St 59 E3
Colebrooke Ter 59 E3
College St 64 B1
Collins St 64 C1
Coll Pl 61 F4
Coll St 61 F4
Columba St 62 B1
Colvend La 64 D5
Colvend St 64 D5
Comelypark Pl 65 E2
 Comelypark St
Comelypark St 64 D2
Commerce St 63 H3
Commercial Ct 64 B3
Commercial Rd 64 A4
Congress Rd 62 D1
Congress Way 63 E1
Connal St 65 F5
Contin Pl 58 D1
Cook St 63 G3
Cooperage Pl 58 C6

Coopers Well La 58 C5
 Dumbarton Rd
Coopers Well St 58 C5
Copland Pl 62 B1
Copland Quad 62 B2
Copland Rd 62 B2
Coplaw Ct 63 G5
Coplaw St 63 G5
Cornhill St 61 E1
Corn St 59 H4
Cornwall St 62 D3
Cornwall St S 62 D4
Corsock St 65 G1
Corston St 61 H6
Corunna St 59 E6
Cotton St 64 D6
Coulin Gdns 60 B2
Couper St 60 B5
Coventry Dr 61 F6
Cowan La 59 E4
Cowan St 59 E4
Cowcaddens Rd 59 H5
Cowcaddens St 59 H5
 Renfield St
Cowlairs Rd 60 C2
Coxhill St 60 B3
Craigenbay St 61 F2
Craigendmuir St 61 H4
Craighall Rd 59 H4
Craighead Av 61 H3
Craigiehall Pl 62 D2
Craigiehall St 62 D2
 Craigiehall Pl
Craigielea St 61 E6
Craigie St 63 G6
Craigmaddie 59 E5
 Ter La
 Derby St
Craigmont Dr 59 E1
Craigmore St 65 G2
Craignethan Gdns 58 B4
 Lawrie St
Craigpark 65 E1
Craigpark Dr 65 E1
Craigpark Ter 65 E1
 Craigpark
Crail St 65 H3
Cramond St 64 B6
Cranborne Rd 58 A1
Cranston St 59 F6
Cranworth La 58 D3
Cranworth St 58 D3
Crathie Dr 58 A4
Crathie La 58 A4
 Exeter Dr
Crawford La 58 A4
 Crawford St
Crawford Path 58 A4
 Crawford St
Crawford St 58 A4
Cresswell La 58 D3
Cresswell St 58 D3
Crichton Pl 60 C2
Crichton St 60 C2
 Crichton St
Crieff Ct 59 F6
 North St
Crimea St 63 G1
Crinan St 61 F6
Croftbank St 60 D2
Cromer Gdns 59 F1
Cromwell La 59 G4
Cromwell St 59 G4
Crown Circ 58 C3
Crown St 64 A1
 Virginia St
Crown Gdns 58 C3
Crown Mans 58 B3
 North Gardner St
Crownpoint Rd 64 D3
Crown Rd N 58 B3
Crown Rd S 58 B3
Crown St 64 A3
Crown Ter 58 B3
Crow Rd 58 A3

Croy Pl 61 G1
Croy Rd 61 G1
Cubie St 64 D3
Culloden St 61 F6
Cumberland Arc 64 A4
 Sandyfaulds Sq
Cumberland Pl 64 A4
Cumberland St 63 H3
Cumbernauld Rd 65 F1
Custom Ho Quay 64 A2
 Clyde St
Cuthbertson St 63 G6
Cuthelton St 65 H4
Cuthelton Ter 65 H4
Cypress St 60 B1

D
Dalcross La 58 C4
 Byres Rd
Dalcross Pas 58 C4
 Dalcross St
Dalcross St 58 C4
Dale Path 64 D4
Dale St 64 D4
Dalhousie La 59 G5
 Dalhousie St
Dalhousie St 59 G5
Dalintober St 63 G3
Dalkeith Av 62 B4
Dalmally St 59 F3
Dalmarnock Br 65 F6
Dalmarnock Ct 65 F5
Dalmarnock Rd 64 D4
Dalmeny St 64 C6
Dalnair St 58 C5
Dalriada St 65 G4
Dalserf Ct 65 F3
Dalserf Gdns 65 F3
Dalserf St 65 F3
Dalziel Dr 62 C5
Dalziel Quad 62 C5
Dargarvel Av 62 B4
Dargarvel Path 62 A5
 Dumbreck Av
Darnick St 61 F3
Darnley Gdns 63 E6
Darnley Pl 63 E6
 Darnley Rd
Darnley Rd 63 E6
Darnley St 63 F6
Dartford St 59 H3
Davaar St 65 F4
Dava St 62 A1
Davidson St 65 E6
David St 65 E3
Dawson Pl 59 H3
Dawson Rd 59 H3
Deanside La 64 B1
 Rottenrow
Dechmont St 65 G3
Dee St 61 H5
Denham St 59 H3
Denmark St 60 A2
Derby St 59 E6
Derby Ter La 59 E5
Derwent St 59 H2
Deveron St 61 H5
Devon Pl 63 H4
Devonshire 58 B2
 Gdns
Devonshire 58 B2
 Gdns La
 Hyndland Rd
Devonshire Ter 58 B2
Devonshire Ter La 58 B2
Devon St 63 H4
Dick St 59 F3
Dinart St 61 H5
Dinwiddie St 61 G4
Dixons Blazes 64 A5
 Ind Est
Dixon St 63 H2
Dobbies Ln 59 H5
Dobbies Ln Pl 60 B6
Dolphin Rd 62 D6

Doncaster St 59 G2
Don St 61 H6
Dora St 64 D5
Dornoch St 64 D3
Dorset Sq 59 F6
 Dorset St
Dorset St 59 F6
Douglas La 59 G6
 West Regent St
Douglas St 59 G6
Douglas Ter 63 F5
 Glencairn Dr
Doune Gdns 59 E3
Doune Gdns La 59 E3
Doune Quad 59 E3
Dover St 59 E6
Dowanhill St 58 C3
Dowanside La 58 D3
 Byres Rd
Dowanside Rd 58 C3
Downiebrae Rd 65 F6
Downs St 60 D2
Drake St 64 C3
Dreghorn St 65 G1
Drem Pl 58 B4
 Merkland St
Drumbottie Rd 61 E1
Drumpellier St 61 H4
Drury St 63 H1
 Renfield St
Dryburgh Gdns 59 F3
 Wilton St
Drygate 64 C1
Duchray La 61 H5
Duchray St 61 H5
Dudley Dr 58 A3
Dudley La 58 A3
Duke St 64 C1
Dumbarton Rd 58 A4
Dumbreck Av 62 A4
Dumbreck Ct 62 A5
Dumbreck Path 62 A4
 Dumbreck Av
Dumbreck Pl 62 A5
Dumbreck Rd 62 B5
Dumbreck Sq 62 A4
Dunard St 59 F2
Dunaskin St 58 C5
Dunbeith Pl 58 D1
Dunblane St 59 H5
Dunchattan Pl 64 D1
Dunchattan St 64 D1
Dunclutha St 65 F6
Dundashill 59 H4
Dundas La 60 A6
Dundas St 60 A6
Dundasvale Ct 59 H5
 Maitland St
Dundasvale Rd 59 H5
 Maitland St
Dundonald Rd 58 C2
Dunearn St 59 F4
Dunkeld St 65 G4
Dunlop St 64 A2
Dunmore La 63 H3
 Norfolk St
Dunmore St 64 A3
Dunn St 65 E4
Dunolly St 61 E5
Dunragit St 65 G1
Dunrobin St 65 F2
Dunsmuir St 62 B1
Duntroon St 61 F6
Durham St 62 D3
Dyce La 58 A4
Dyer's La 64 B2
Dykemuir Pl 61 F2
 Dykemuir St
Dykemuir Quad 61 E2
 Dykemuir St
Dykemuir St 61 E2

E
Eaglesham Ct 63 E2
 Blackburn St

Name	Ref		Name	Ref		Name	Ref		Name	Ref		Name	Ref
Eaglesham Pl	63 E2		Fergus Ct	59 E2		Garrioch Cres	58 D1		Govanhill St	63 H6		Hayburn Ct	58 B4
Eagle St	60 A4		*Fergus Dr*			Garrioch Dr	58 D1		Govan Rd	62 C2		*Hayburn St*	
Earlston Av	60 D5		Fergus Dr	59 E2		Garrioch Gate	59 E1		Gower La	62 D3		Hayburn Cres	58 A3
Earlston Pl	60 C5		Fergus La	59 F2		*Garrioch Rd*			*North Gower St*			Hayburn Gate	58 B4
Earnock St	61 H2		Fernbank St	60 C1		Garriochmill Rd	59 E2		Gower St	62 C4		Hayburn La	58 A3
East Bath La	60 A6		Ferry Rd	58 B5		Garriochmill Way	59 F3		Gower Ter	62 C3		Hayburn Pl	58 B4
Sauchiehall St			Fielden Pl	65 E3		*South Woodside Rd*			Grace St	63 F1		*Hayburn St*	
Eastburn Rd	61 F1		Fielden St	65 E3		Garrioch Quad	58 D1		Grafton Pl	60 A6		Hayburn St	58 B5
East Campbell St	64 C2		Findhorn St	61 H6		Garrioch Rd	58 D2		Graham Sq	64 D2		Hayfield Ct	64 B4
Eastcroft Ter	61 E2		Finlas St	60 B2		Garscube Cross	59 H4		Graignestock Pl	64 C3		Hayfield St	64 B4
Eastercraigs	61 F6		Finlay Dr	61 E1		Garscube Rd	59 G3		*London Rd*			Hayston Cres	59 H1
Eastfield Rd	60 C2		Finnart Sq	64 D5		Gartferry St	60 D2		Graignestock St	64 C3		Hayston St	59 H1
Eastvale Pl	58 C6		Finnart St	64 D5		Garthland Dr	65 E1		Granby La	58 D3		Hazelwood Rd	62 C4
East Wellington St	65 H3		Finnieston Quay	63 E1		Garth St	64 A1		Granton St	64 C6		Heddle Pl	63 G1
East Whitby St	65 G4		Finnieston Sq	59 E6		Gartness St	65 F1		Grant St	59 F5		*Cadogan St*	
Eccles St	60 C1		*Finnieston St*			Gartons Rd	61 G1		Granville St	59 F6		Helen St	62 A1
Carron St			Finnieston St	63 E1		Garvald Ct	65 E6		Gray St	59 E5		Helenvale Ct	65 H4
Edelweiss Ter	58 B4		Firhill Rd	59 G2		*Baltic St*			Great Dovehill	64 B2		Helenvale St	65 G4
Gardner St			Firhill St	59 G2		Garvald St	65 F5		Great George St	58 D3		Henderson St	59 F3
Eden La	61 H5		Firpark Pl	60 D6		Gateside St	65 F2		Great Kelvin La	59 E4		Herbert St	59 F3
Eden St	61 H5		*Firpark St*			Gear Ter	65 F6		Great Western Rd	59 E3		Heron St	64 D4
Edgefauld Av	60 D3		Firpark St	60 D6		General Terminus	63 F2		Great Western Ter	58 C2		Herries Rd	63 F5
Edgefauld Dr	60 D2		Firpark Ter	64 D1		Quay			Great Western Ter	58 C2		Herriet St	63 F5
Edgefauld Pl	60 D1		First Gdns	62 A4		George Sq	64 A1		La			Hickman Ter	64 A6
Edgefauld Rd	60 D2		Fisher Ct	64 D1		George St	64 A1		Green, The	64 C3		Hickory St	60 C1
Edgehill La	58 A2		Fitzroy La	59 E6		Gibson St	59 E4		Greendyke St	64 B2		Highburgh Rd	58 C3
Edinburgh Rd	65 H1		Fitzroy Pl	59 E5		(Hillhead)			Greenhead St	64 C4		High Craighall Rd	59 H4
Edington St	59 H4		*Royal Ter*			Gibson St	64 C2		Greenlodge Ter	64 C4		Highland La	58 C6
Edwin St	62 D3		Fleming St	65 F2		(Calton)			*Greenhead St*			High St	64 B2
Eglinton Ct	63 H3		Flemington St	60 D3		Gilbert St	58 C6		Greenrig St	61 H3		Hillfoot St	65 E1
Eglinton St	63 H3		Fleurs Av	62 B4		Gilmour Pl	64 A4		Green St	64 C3		Hillhead Pl	59 E4
Elba La	65 G3		Fleurs Rd	62 B4		Girvan St	61 H5		Gretna St	65 F4		*Bank St*	
Gallowgate			Florence St	64 A3		Gladstone St	59 G4		Grier Path	65 H3		Hillhead St	58 D4
Elcho St	64 D2		Forbes Dr	64 D3		Glamis Rd	65 H4		*Crail St*			Hillhouse St	61 E2
Elderslie St	59 F5		Forbes St	64 D2		Glasgow Br	63 H2		Grierson La	61 H6		Hillkirk Pl	60 C2
Eldon Ct	58 B4		Fordneuk St	65 E3		Glasgow Cross	64 B2		*Lomax St*			*Hillkirk St*	
Caird Dr			Ford Rd	58 D2		Glasgow Grn	64 B3		Grierson St	61 H6		Hillkirk St	60 C2
Eldon St	59 E4		Fordyce St	58 B4		Glasgow St	59 E3		Grosvenor Cres	58 D3		Hillkirk St La	60 D2
Elgin St	65 E3		Foremount Ter La	58 B3		Glassford St	64 A1		Grosvenor Cres	58 D3		*Hillkirk St*	
Rowchester St			Foresthall Cres	61 E3		Glebe Ct	60 B6		La			Hillsborough Ter	59 E3
Elie St	58 C4		Foresthall Dr	61 E3		Glebe St	60 B5		*Byres Rd*			*Bower St*	
Elizabeth St	62 C3		Forge Pl	61 F4		Glenapp St	63 F5		Grosvenor La	58 D3		Hillside Gdns La	58 B3
Ellesmere St	59 G2		Forge Retail Pk	65 F2		Glenbarr St	60 D5		Grosvenor Ter	58 D3		*North Gardner St*	
Elliot Pl	59 E6		Forge Shop Cen,	65 G3		Glencairn Dr	62 D6		Grovepark Ct	59 G4		Hill St	59 G5
Finnieston St			The			Glencairn Gdns	62 D6		Grovepark Gdns	59 G4		Hinshaw St	59 G3
Elliot St	63 E1		Forge St	61 F4		Glencairn La	63 F6		Grovepark Pl	59 G3		Hinshelwood Dr	62 A2
Elmbank Cres	59 G6		Forrestfield St	61 E5		Glendale Pl	65 F2		Grovepark St	59 G3		Hobart St	59 H2
Elmbank La	59 F6		Forrest St	65 E3		Glendale St	65 F2		Gullane St	58 B5		Hobden St	61 E3
North St			Forth St	63 F5		Glendarvel Gdns	60 B2		*Anderson St*			Hogarth Av	65 H1
Elmbank St	59 G6		Fortrose St	58 B4		Glenfarg St	59 G4					Hogarth Cres	65 H1
Elmbank St La	59 G6		Fotheringay La	62 D6		Glenisla St	65 H5		**H**			Hogarth Dr	65 H1
Elmfoot St	64 B6		Fotheringay Rd	62 D6		Glenmavis St	59 H5		Haggswood Av	62 C6		Hogarth Gdns	65 H1
Elmvale Row	60 C1		Foundry St	60 D2		Glenpark Rd	65 F2		Haghill Rd	65 G2		Hogganfield Ct	61 H4
Elmvale Row E	60 C1		Fountain St	64 C2		Glenpark St	65 F2		Haig St	60 D2		Hogganfield St	61 H4
Elmvale Row			Fountainwell Av	60 B3		Glenshee Ct	65 H5		Hallside Pl	64 A4		Holland St	59 G6
Elmvale Row W	60 C1		Fountainwell Dr	60 B4		Glenshee St	65 H5		Hamilton Av	62 D5		Hollybank St	61 E5
Elmvale Row			Fountainwell Pl	60 B4		Glentrool Gdns	60 A2		Hamilton Dr	59 E3		Hollybrook Pl	64 A6
Elmvale St	60 C1		Fountainwell Rd	60 B4		Gloucester St	63 G3		Hamiltonhill Cres	59 H2		*Hollybrook St*	
Elphinstone Pl	62 C1		Fountainwell Sq	60 C4		Golfhill Dr	61 E6		*Hamiltonhill Rd*			Hollybrook St	64 A6
Eltham St	59 H3		Fountainwell Ter	60 C4		Golfhill Ter	60 D6		Hamiltonhill Rd	59 H3		Holly Dr	61 E3
Bonhill St			Fourth Gdns	62 A4		Golspie St	58 A6		Hamilton Pk Av	59 E3		Holm St	63 G1
Endrick St	60 B3		Fox St	63 H2		Goosedubbs	64 A2		Handel Pl	64 A4		Holyrood Cres	59 F4
Errol Gdns	64 A4		Foyers Ter	61 E2		*Stockwell St*			Hanover St	64 A1		Holyrood Quad	59 F4
Erskine Av	62 B4		Francis St	63 G4		Gorbals Cross	64 A3		Hanson St	60 D6		Holywell St	65 F3
Esmond St	58 C5		Frankfield St	61 H4		Gorbals La	63 H2		Harcourt Dr	61 F6		Hopefield Av	58 C1
Eton La	59 E4		Franklin St	64 D5		*Oxford St*			Harley St	62 C3		Hopehill Gdns	59 G3
Ewing Pl	65 G3		Frazer St	65 E3		Gorbals St	63 H4		Harmony Ct	62 A1		Hopehill Rd	59 G3
Exchange Pl	64 A1		French St	64 D5		Gordon La	63 H1		Harmony Pl	62 A1		Hope St	63 H1
Buchanan St			Fruin Pl	60 A2		*Mitchell St*			Harmony Row	62 A1		Hopetoun Ter	61 E3
Exeter Dr	58 A4		Fruin St	60 A2		Gordon St	63 H1		Harmony Sq	62 A1		Horne St	60 C1
Exeter La	58 A4					Gorstan Pl	58 C1		*Harmony Row*			*Hawthorn St*	
Exeter Dr			**G**			*Wyndford Rd*			Harrison Dr	62 B2		Hornshill St	61 E2
			Gadie St	61 H6		Gough St	61 H6		*Copland Rd*			Horselethill Rd	58 C3
F			Gadshill St	60 D5		Gourlay Path	60 B3		Harvey St	60 D6		Hospital St	64 A3
Fairbairn Path	65 E4		Gailes St	65 F4		*Endrick St*			Harvie St	62 D2		Hotspur St	59 E1
Ruby St			Gallowgate	64 B2		Gourlay St	60 B3		Hastie St	58 D5		Houldsworth La	59 E6
Fairbairn St	65 E4		Gardner St	58 B4		Gourock St	63 G4		Hathaway La	59 E1		Houldsworth St	59 E6
Fairley St	62 B2		Garfield St	65 E2		*Eglinton St*			Hathaway St	59 E1		Houston Pl	63 F2
Fairlie Pk Dr	58 A4		Garmouth Ct	58 A6		Govan Cross	58 A6		Haugh Rd	58 D6		Houston St	63 F3
Falfield St	63 G4		Garnet Ct	59 G5		*Govan Rd*			Havelock La	58 C4		Howard St	63 H2
Falkland La	58 B3		*New City Rd*			Govan Cross	58 A6		Havelock St	58 C4		Howat St	58 A6
Falkland St	58 B3		Garnethill St	59 G5		Shop Cen			Hawthorn	60 A1		Hughenden Dr	58 B2
Farm Rd	62 B3		Garnet St	59 G5					Quad			Hughenden Gdns	58 A2
Farnell St	59 H4		Garnkirk St	60 C5					Hawthorn St	60 A1		Hughenden La	58 B2
Fauldhouse St	64 B5		Garnock St	60 D4								Hughenden Rd	58 B2

Name	Ref
Hughenden Ter	58 B2
Hughenden Rd	
Hugo St	59 F1
Hunter St	64 C2
Huntingdon Rd	60 C4
Huntingdon Sq	60 C4
Huntly Gdns	58 C3
Huntly Rd	58 C3
Hutcheson St	64 A1
Hutchinsontown Ct	64 A4
Hydepark St	63 F1
Hyndland Av	58 B4
Hyndland Rd	58 B2
Hyndland St	58 C4
I	
Ibroxholm Av	62 B3
Ibroxholm Oval	62 B3
Ibroxholm Pl	62 B3
Paisley Rd W	
Ibrox Ind Est	62 C2
Ibrox St	62 C2
Ibrox Ter	62 B2
Ibrox Ter La	62 B2
India St	59 G6
Ingleby Dr	65 E1
Inglefield St	63 H5
Inglis St	65 E2
Ingram St	64 A1
Inverleith St	65 H2
Invershin Dr	58 D1
Inverurie St	60 B3
Iona St	62 B1
Irongray St	65 G1
Irvine St	65 F5
J	
Jamaica St	63 H2
James Morrison St	64 B2
St. Andrews Sq	
James Nisbet St	60 C6
James St	64 C4
James Watt La	63 G1
James Watt St	
James Watt St	63 G1
Jamieson Ct	63 H6
Jamieson Path	63 H6
Jamieson St	
Jamieson St	63 H6
Janefield St	65 F3
Jardine St	59 F3
Raeberry St	
Jedburgh Gdns	59 F3
Wilton St	
Jessie St	64 B6
Jocelyn Sq	64 A2
John Knox La	64 C1
Drygate	
John Knox St	64 C1
John St	64 A1
Julian Av	58 C2
Julian La	58 C2
K	
Karol Path	59 G4
St. Peters St	
Kay St	60 D2
Keir St	63 F5
Keith Ct	58 C5
Keith St	58 C4
Kelbourne St	59 E2
Kellas St	62 A1
Kelty Pl	63 H3
Bedford St	
Kelvin Dr	58 D2
Kelvingrove St	59 E6
Kelvinhaugh Gate	58 D6
Kelvinhaugh St	
Kelvinhaugh Pl	58 D6
Kelvinhaugh St	
Kelvinhaugh St	58 C6
Kelvinside Av	59 E2
Kelvinside Dr	59 F2
Kelvinside Gdns	59 E2
Kelvinside Gdns E	59 F3
Kelvinside Gdns La	59 E2
Kelvinside Ter S	59 E3
Kelvinside Ter W	59 E3
Kelvin Way	58 D5
Kempock St	65 G4
Kemp St	60 C2
Kenmure St	63 F6
Kennedy Path	60 B6
St. Mungo Pl	
Kennedy St	60 B5
Kennet St	61 E5
Kennyhill Sq	61 F6
Kensington Gate	58 C2
Kensington Rd	
Kensington Gate La	58 C2
Kensington Rd	58 C2
Kent Rd	59 E6
Kent St	64 C2
Keppochhill Dr	60 B4
Keppochhill Pl	60 B4
Keppochhill Rd	60 A3
Keppochhill Way	60 B3
Keppoch St	60 B3
Kerr Dr	64 D3
Kerr Pl	64 D3
Kerr St	64 D3
Kerrydale St	65 F4
Kersland La	58 D3
Kersland St	58 D3
Kessock Dr	59 H3
Kessock Pl	59 H3
Kew Gdns	58 D3
Ruthven St	
Kew La	58 D3
Kew Ter	58 D3
Kidston Pl	64 A4
Kidston Ter	64 A4
Kilbarchan St	63 H3
Bedford St	
Kilberry St	61 E5
Kilbirnie Pl	63 G4
Kilbirnie St	63 G4
Kilbride St	64 B6
Kildonan Dr	58 A4
Kildrostan St	63 F6
Killearn St	59 H2
Killermont St	60 A6
Killiegrew Rd	62 D6
Kilmair Pl	58 D1
Kinbuck St	60 B2
Kingarth La	63 G6
Kingarth St	63 G6
King George V Br	63 H2
Kingsborough Gdns	58 B3
Kingsborough Gate	58 B3
Prince Albert Rd	
Kingsborough La	58 B3
Kingsborough La E	58 B3
King's Br	64 B4
Kings Cross	64 D1
King's Dr	64 C4
Kingston Br	63 G2
Kingston Ind Est	63 G3
Kingston St	63 G2
King St	64 A2
Kinloch St	65 G4
Kinnear Rd	65 F5
Kinning Pk Ind Est	63 F3
Kinning St	63 G3
Kinnoul La	58 C3
Dowanside Rd	
Kintra St	62 B1
Kintyre St	61 E5
Kirkcaldy Rd	62 D6
Kirkhill Dr	59 E1
Kirkhill Pl	58 D1
Kirkhill Dr	
Kirkland St	59 F3
Kirklee Circ	58 C2
Kirklee Gdns	58 C1
Kirklee Gdns La	58 D2
Kirklee Gate	58 D2
Kirklee Pl	58 D2
Kirklee Quad	58 D2
Kirklee Quad La	58 D2
Kirklee Quad	
Kirklee Rd	58 C2
Kirklee Ter	58 C2
Kirklee Ter La	58 C2
Kirkmichael Av	58 A3
Blairatholl Av	
Kirkmichael Gdns	58 A3
Blairatholl Av	
Kirkpatrick St	65 E3
Kirkwood St	62 C3
Knowehead Gdns	63 E5
Knowehead Ter	
Knowehead Ter	63 E5
Kyle St	60 A5
L	
La Belle Allee	59 E5
La Belle Pl	59 E5
Laburnum Rd	62 C4
La Crosse Ter	59 E3
Ladywell St	64 C1
Laidlaw St	63 G3
Laird Pl	64 D4
Lambhill Quad	63 E3
Lambhill St	62 D3
Lanark St	64 B2
Lancaster Cres	58 C2
Lancaster Cres La	58 C2
Lancaster Ter	58 C2
Lancaster Ter La	58 C2
Westbourne Gdns W	
Lancefield Quay	63 E1
Lancefield St	63 F1
Landressy Pl	64 C4
Landressy St	64 D4
Lane Gdns	58 B3
North Gardner St	
Langbank St	63 H3
Eglinton St	
Langrig Rd	61 E2
Langshot St	62 D3
Lansdowne Cres	59 F4
Lansdowne Cres La	59 F4
Larbert St	59 H5
Larch Rd	62 B3
Largs St	65 F1
Latherton Dr	58 D1
Latherton Pl	58 D1
Latherton Dr	
Laudedale La	58 B3
Lauderdale Gdns	58 B3
Laurel Pl	58 A3
Laurel St	58 A4
Laurieston Rd	63 H4
Laverockhall St	60 D3
Lawmoor Av	64 A5
Lawmoor Pl	64 A6
Lawmoor Rd	64 A5
Lawmoor St	64 A5
Lawrence St	58 C4
Lawrie St	58 B4
Law St	65 E3
Leadburn Rd	61 G2
Leader St	61 H5
Ledaig Pl	65 G1
Ledaig St	65 G1
Leicester Av	58 B1
Leith St	61 H6
Lendel Pl	62 D3
Paisley Rd W	
Leny St	59 F2
Lenzie St	60 D1
Lenzie Ter	60 D1
Leslie Rd	63 E5
Leslie St	63 F5
Lettoch St	62 A1
Leven St	63 F5
Leyden Ct	59 E1
Leyden Gdns	59 E1
Leyden St	59 E1
Liberton St	61 H6
Lightburn Rd	65 G2
Lilybank Gdns	58 D4
Lilybank Gdns La	58 D4
Lilybank La	58 D4
Lilybank Gdns	
Lilybank Ter	58 D4
Great George St	
Lily St	65 F5
Lincluden Path	63 F4
McCulloch St	
Linfern Rd	58 C3
Lismore Rd	58 B1
Lister St	60 B5
Little Dovehill	64 B2
Gallowgate	
Little St	63 F1
McIntyre St	
Lloyd St	61 E6
Lochgreen St	61 H3
Lockhart St	61 F4
Logan St	64 B5
Lomax St	61 H6
Lomond St	59 H1
London Arc	64 B2
London Rd	
London La	64 B2
London Rd	
London Rd	64 B2
Longford St	61 H6
Lorne St	62 D2
Lorraine Gdns	58 C2
Kensington Rd	
Lorraine Gdns La	58 C2
Westbourne Gdns La	
Lorraine Rd	58 C2
Kensington Rd	
Lossie St	61 H5
Lothian Gdns	59 E3
Wilton St	
Loudon Ter	58 D3
Observatory Rd	
Lovat St	60 A4
Borron St	
Lowther Ter	58 C2
Redlands La	
Luath St	58 A6
Lumloch St	61 E2
Lumsden St	58 D6
Lymburn St	58 D5
Lyndhurst Gdns	59 E3
Lyndhurst Gdns La	59 E2
Lynedoch Cres	59 F5
Lynedoch Cres La	59 F5
Lynedoch Pl	59 F5
Lynedoch St	59 F5
Lynedoch Ter	59 F5
M	
McAlpine St	63 G1
McAslin Ct	60 B6
McAslin St	60 C6
Macbeth Pl	65 H4
Macbeth St	65 H4
McCulloch St	63 F4
Macduff Pl	65 H4
Macduff St	65 H4
McFarlane St	64 C2
McIntosh Ct	64 D1
McIntosh St	64 D1
McIntyre St	63 F1
McKechnie St	58 A6
Mackeith St	64 D4
Mackie St	60 A4
Borron St	
Mackinlay St	63 H4
Maclean Sq	62 D2
Maclean St	62 D2
Maclellan St	62 D3
Macleod St	60 C6
McNeil Gdns	64 B4
McNeil St	64 B4
McPhail St	64 C4
McPhater St	59 H5
Madras Pl	64 D5
Madras St	64 D5
Mafeking St	62 B2
Main St	64 D5
Mair St	63 E2
Maitland St	59 H5
Malloch St	59 E1
Malta Ter	63 H4
Maltbarns St	59 G3
Malvern Ct	65 E2
Manresa Pl	59 H4
Mansel St	60 D1
Mansfield St	58 C4
Mansion St	60 A1
Maple Rd	62 B4
March La	63 F6
Nithsdale Dr	
Marchmont Ter	58 C3
Observatory Rd	
March St	63 F6
Marine Cres	63 E2
Marine Gdns	63 F2
Mavisbank Gdns	
Mariscat Rd	63 E6
Marlow St	63 E4
Marne St	65 F1
Martha St	60 A6
Martin St	64 D5
Mart St	64 A2
Bridgegate	
Marwick St	65 F1
Maryhill Rd	59 F3
Maryhill Shop Cen	59 E1
Maryston Pl	61 H4
Maryston St	61 H4
Mary St	59 H4
Marywood Sq	63 F6
Masterton St	60 A3
Mathieson St	64 B4
Matilda Rd	63 E5
Mauchline St	63 G4
Maukinfauld Ct	65 H5
Mauldslie St	65 H4
Maule Dr	58 A4
Mavisbank Gdns	63 E2
Maxwell Av	63 E4
Maxwell Ct	63 E4
St. John's Rd	
Maxwell Dr	62 C4
Maxwell Gdns	62 D4
Maxwell Gro	62 D4
Maxwell La	63 E4
Maxwell Dr	
Maxwell Oval	63 F4
Maxwell Pl	63 G5
Maxwell Rd	63 F4
Maxwell St	64 A2
Maxwell Ter	63 E4
Maxwelton Rd	61 H4
Meadowpark St	65 F1
Meadow Rd	58 A5
Meadowside St	58 A5
Megan Gate	64 D4
Megan St	
Megan St	64 D4
Melbourne St	64 D2
Meldrum Gdns	62 D6
Melfort Av	59 F3
Melrose Gdns	59 F3
Melrose St	59 F4
Queens Cres	
Melvaig Pl	58 D1
Melville Ct	64 B2
Brunswick St	
Melville St	63 F5
Memel St	60 C1
Menzies Dr	61 E1
Menzies Pl	61 E1
Menzies Rd	61 E1
Merchant La	64 A2
Merkland Ct	58 B5
Vine St	

Merkland St 58 B4
Merrick Gdns 62 B3
Merrick Path 62 B3
Merrick Gdns
Merryland Pl 62 B1
Merryland St 62 B1
Methven St 65 H5
Metropole La 64 A2
Clyde St
Middlesex Gdns 63 E2
Middlesex St 63 E3
Middleton St 62 C2
Midland St 63 H1
Midlock St 62 C3
Midton St 60 D3
Midwharf St 60 A4
Migvie Pl 58 D1
Wyndford Rd
Milan St 63 G5
Millarbank St 60 C2
Millburn St 60 D5
Mill Cres 64 D5
Millcroft Rd 64 D6
Millerfield Pl 65 F5
Millerfield Rd 65 F5
Millerston St 65 E2
Miller St 64 A1
Millroad Dr 64 C2
Millroad Gdns 64 D2
Millroad St 64 C2
Mill St 64 D5
Milnbank St 61 E6
Milnpark Gdns 62 D3
Milnpark St 63 E3
Milton St 60 A5
Minerva St 59 E6
Minerva Way 59 E6
Mingarry La 59 E2
Clouston St
Mingarry St 59 E2
Mireton St 59 H1
Mirrlees Dr 58 C2
Mirrlees La 58 C2
Mitchell La 63 H1
Mitchell St 63 H1
Moffat St 64 B4
Moir St 64 B2
Molendinar Gdns 61 H4
Molendinar St 64 B2
Mollinsburn St 60 C3
Monar Dr 59 H3
Monar St
Monar Pl 59 H3
Monar St
Monar St 59 H3
Monart Pl 59 F1
Moncur St 64 C2
Monkscroft Av 58 A3
Monkscroft Ct 58 A4
Crow Rd
Monkscroft Gdns 58 A3
Monkscroft Av
Montague La 58 B2
Montague St 59 F4
Monteith Row 64 C3
Monteith Row La 64 C3
Monteith Pl
Montgomery St 65 E4
Montrose St 60 B6
Moodiesburn St 61 H4
Moore St 64 D2
Gallowgate
Moray Pl 63 E6
Mordaunt St 65 E5
Morgan Ms 63 H5
Morningside St 61 H6
Morrin Path 60 C2
Crichton St
Morrin Sq 60 C6
Collins St
Morrin St 60 C2
Morrison St 63 G2
Mosesfield St 60 D1
Mosque Av 64 A3

Mountainblue St 65 E3
Mount St 59 F3
Moy St 58 C4
Church St
Muirhead St 58 B4
Purdon St
Muirpark St 58 B4
Gardner St
Mull St 61 F4
Murano St 59 F2
Murdoch St 60 D1
Lenzie St
Muslin St 64 D4
Myreside Pl 65 H2
Myreside St 65 H2

N

Naburn Gate 64 A4
Nairn St 58 D5
Nansen St 59 G3
Napier Dr 58 B6
Napier Pl 58 B6
Napier Rd 58 B6
Napiershall La 59 F4
Napiershall Pl 59 F4
Napiershall St
Napiershall St 59 F4
Napier St 58 B6
Napier Ter 58 B6
Nelson Mandela 60 A6
Pl
Nelson St 63 G2
Neptune St 62 B1
Nethan St 58 A6
Netherby Dr 62 D4
Netherfield St 65 G2
Newark Dr 62 D5
Newbank Gdns 65 H4
New City Rd 59 H5
Newhall St 64 C5
Newmill Rd 61 G1
Newton Pl 59 F5
Newton St 59 G6
Argyle St
Newton Ter 59 F6
Sauchiehall St
Newton Ter La 59 F6
New Wynd 64 A2
Nicholas St 64 B1
Nicholson La 63 H2
Nicholson St
Nicholson St 63 H2
Niddrie Rd 63 F6
Niddrie Sq 63 F6
Nisbet St 65 H3
Nithsdale Dr 63 F6
Nithsdale Pl 63 F5
Nithsdale Rd
Nithsdale Rd 63 F6
Nithsdale St 63 F6
Nith St 61 H5
Norfolk Ct 63 H3
Norfolk La 63 H3
Norfolk St
Norfolk St 64 A3
Norman St 64 D5
North Canal Bk 60 A4
North Canal Bk St 60 A4
North Claremont 59 E5
St
Royal Ter
North Ct 64 A1
St. Vincent Pl
North Ct La 64 A1
Buchanan St
Northcroft Rd 60 D2
North Frederick St 64 A1
North Gardner St 58 B4
North Gower St 62 C3
North Hanover Pl 60 A6
North Hanover St
North Hanover St 60 A6
Northpark St 59 F2
North Pl 59 F6
North St

North Portland St 64 B1
North St 59 F6
Northumberland 59 E2
St
North Wallace St 60 B5
North Woodside 59 F3
Rd
Norval St 58 A4
Norwich Dr 58 B1
Novar Dr 58 A2
Nuneaton St 65 E5
Nuneaton St 65 E5
Ind Est
Nursery La 63 F6
Nursery St 63 G5
Pollokshaws Rd

O

Oakbank Ind Est 59 H3
Oakfield Av 59 E4
Oakfield La 59 E4
Oakley Ter 64 D1
Oak St 63 G1
Oatfield St 61 F2
Oban Ct 59 E2
Kelvinside Gdns
Oban Dr 59 E2
Oban La 59 E2
Observatory La 58 D3
Observatory Rd
Observatory Rd 58 C3
Ogilvie Pl 65 H4
Ogilvie St 65 H4
Old Dalmarnock 64 D4
Rd
Old Dumbarton 58 C5
Rd
Old Rutherglen 64 A4
Rd
Old Wynd 64 A2
Olive St 61 H2
Olympia St 64 D3
Onslow Dr 65 E1
Onslow Sq 65 E1
Oran Gdns 59 E1
Oran Gate 59 E1
Oran Pl 59 E2
Oran St 59 E1
Oregon Pl 64 A4
Orkney Pl 62 A1
Orkney St
Orkney St 62 B1
Orr Pl 64 D2
Orr St 64 D3
Osborne St 64 A2
Oswald St 63 H2
Otago La 59 E4
Otago La N 59 E4
Otago St 59 E4
Overnewton Pl 58 D6
Kelvinhaugh St
Overnewton Sq 58 D5
Blackie St
Overnewton St 58 D5
Overtown Pl 65 E3
Overtown St 65 E3
Oxford La 63 H3
Oxford St 63 H2

P

Pacific Dr 62 C2
Pacific Quay 62 D1
Paisley Rd 63 G2
Paisley Rd W 62 C3
Palermo St 60 C2
Atlas Rd
Palmerston Pl 58 D6
Kelvinhaugh St
Panmure St 59 G2
Park Av 59 F4
Park Circ 59 E5
Park Circ La 59 E5
Park Circ Pl 59 F5
Park Dr 59 E4
Park Gdns 59 E5

Park Gdns La 59 E5
Park Gate 59 E5
Parkgrove Ter 59 E5
Parkgrove Ter La 59 E5
Derby St
Parkhead Cross 65 H3
Park Quad 59 E5
Park Rd 59 E4
Park St S 59 E5
Park Ter 59 E5
Park Ter E La 59 E5
Park Ter La 59 E5
Parnie St 64 A2
Parsonage Row 64 B1
Parsonage Sq 64 B1
Parson St 60 C6
Partick Br St 58 C4
Partickhill Av 58 B4
Partickhill Ct 58 B3
Partickhill Rd 58 B3
Paterson St 63 G3
Patna St 65 F5
Paton St 65 F1
Payne St 60 A4
Pearce La 58 A6
Pearce St
Pearce St 58 A6
Peathill St 60 A3
Peel La 58 B4
Peel St 58 B4
Pembroke St 59 F6
Penicuik St 65 H2
Percy St 62 D2
Clifford St
Perth St 63 F1
Argyle St
Petershill Ct 61 G2
Petershill Dr 61 F2
Petershill Pl 61 F2
Petershill Rd 60 D3
Phoenix Pk Ter 59 H4
Corn St
Phoenix Rd 59 G5
Great Western Rd
Piccadilly St 63 F1
Pine Pl 64 A4
Pinkston Dr 60 C4
Pinkston Rd 60 B3
Pitt St 63 G1
Plantation Pk 62 D3
Gdns
Clifford La
Plantation Sq 63 E2
Plant St 65 G2
Playfair St 65 E5
Pointhouse Rd 63 E1
Pollokshaws Rd 63 G6
Pollokshields 63 F6
Glencairn Dr
Polmadie Av 64 B6
Polmadie Ind Est 64 C6
Polmadie Rd 64 C5
Polwarth La 58 B2
Polwarth St 58 B3
Poplar Rd 62 B3
Urrdale Rd
Poplin St 64 D5
Port Dundas 60 A4
Ind Est
Port Dundas Pl 60 A6
Port Dundas Rd 59 H5
Port Dundas 60 A4
Trd Centres
Porter St 62 C3
Clifford St
Portman Pl 59 E4
Cowan St
Portman St 63 E3
Port St 59 F6
Portugal La 63 H3
Bedford St
Portugal St 63 H3
Possil Cross 60 A3
Possil Rd 59 H3
Powfoot St 65 H3

Preston Pl 63 H6
Preston St 63 H6
Prince Albert Rd 58 B3
Prince Edward St 63 G6
Prince's Dock 62 C1
Princes Gdns 58 B3
Princes Pl 58 C3
Princes Sq 64 A1
Buchanan St
Princes Ter 58 C3
Provanhill St 60 D5
Provanmill Pl 61 H3
Provanmill Rd
Provanmill Rd 61 H3
Provan Rd 61 G5
Purdon St 58 B4

Q

Quarrybrae St 65 H3
Quarrywood Av 61 G2
Quarrywood Rd 61 H2
Queen Elizabeth 64 B4
Sq
Queen Margaret 59 E2
Ct
Fergus Dr
Queen Margaret 58 D3
Dr
Queen Margaret 59 E2
Rd
Queen Mary St 64 D4
Queensborough 58 A2
Gdns
Queens Cres 59 F4
Queens Dr 63 F6
Queensferry St 64 C6
Queens Gdns 58 C3
Victoria Cres Rd
Queens Gate La 58 C3
Victoria Cres Rd
Queenslie St 61 H4
Queens Pl 58 C3
Queen Sq 63 F6
Queen St 64 A1

R

Radnor St 58 D5
Argyle St
Raeberry St 59 F3
Rafford St 62 A1
Raglan St 59 G4
Rathlin St 58 A6
Ratho Dr 60 C1
Ravel Row 65 H3
Ravelston St 65 H2
Redan St 64 D3
Redford St 61 H6
Redlands La 58 C2
Redlands Rd 58 C2
Redlands Ter 58 C2
Julian Av
Redlands Ter La 58 C2
Redmoss St 59 H1
Rednock St 60 A2
Red Rd 61 F2
Red Rd Ct 61 F3
Redwood Dr 61 E3
Regent Moray 58 D5
St
Regent Pk Sq 63 F6
Reidhouse St 60 D1
Reid Pl 64 D4
Reid St 64 D5
Reidvale St 64 D2
Renfield La 63 H1
Hope St
Renfield St 63 H1
Renfrew Ct 59 H6
Renfrew La 59 H6
Hope St
Renfrew St 59 H6
Renton St 60 A5
Rhymer St 60 C5
Rhynie Dr 62 B3
Riccarton St 64 A6

Richard St 63 G1
Cadzow St
Richmond St 64 B1
Rimsdale St 65 E3
Ringford St 60 D3
Risk St 64 C3
Ritchie St 63 G4
Riverview Dr 63 G2
Riverview Gdns 63 G2
Riverview Pl 63 G2
Robert Dr 58 A6
Roberton Av 62 C6
Robertson La 63 G1
Robertson St 63 H1
Robert St 58 A6
Robson Gro 63 H5
Rockbank Pl 65 E3
Rockbank St 65 E3
Rockcliffe St 64 D5
Rockfield Pl 61 G1
Rockfield Rd 61 G1
Rock St 59 H3
Rodney St 59 H4
Roebank St 61 F6
Rogart St 64 D3
Rona St 61 F4
Ropework La 64 A2
Clyde St
Roseberry St 64 C5
Rosemount Cres 60 D6
Rosemount St 60 D5
Rose St 59 H6
Rosevale St 58 A4
Roslea Dr 65 E1
Rosneath St 58 A6
Rosslyn Ter 58 C2
Ross St 64 B2
Rosyth Rd 64 C6
Rosyth St 64 C6
Rottenrow 60 B6
Rottenrow E 64 B1
Rowallan Gdns 58 A3
Rowallan La E 58 A3
Rowan Gdns 62 B4
Rowan Rd 62 B4
Rowchester St 65 E3
Roxburgh La 58 D3
Saltoun St
Roxburgh St 58 D3
Royal Bk Pl 64 A1
Buchanan St
Royal Cres 59 E6
Royal Ex Bldgs 64 A1
Royal Ex Sq
Royal Ex Sq 64 A1
Royal Ter 59 E5
Royal Ter La 59 E5
Roystonhill 60 D5
Royston Rd 60 C5
Royston Sq 60 C5
Roy St 60 B3
Ruby St 65 E4
Ruchill Pl 59 F1
Ruchill St
Ruchill St 59 E1
Rumford St 64 D5
Rupert St 59 F4
Rushyhill St 61 E2
Ruskin La 59 E3
Ruskin Pl 59 E3
Great Western Rd
Ruskin Ter 59 E3
Russell St 58 B4
Vine St
Rutherglen Br 64 D5
Rutherglen Rd 64 B5
Ruthven La 58 D3
Ruthven St 58 D3
Rutland Ct 63 E2
Govan Rd
Rutland Cres 63 E2
Rutland Pl 63 E2
Ryebank Rd 61 G1
Rye Cres 61 F1
Ryefield Rd 61 F1

Ryehill Pl 61 G1
Ryehill Rd 61 G1
Ryemount Rd 61 G1
Rye Rd 61 F1
Ryeside Rd 61 F1

S
St. Andrews Cres 63 E4
St. Andrews Cross 63 G5
St. Andrews Dr 63 E4
St. Andrews La 64 B2
Gallowgate
St. Andrews Rd 63 F4
St. Andrews Sq 64 B2
St. Andrews St 64 B2
St. Clair St 59 F4
North Woodside Rd
St. Enoch Pl 63 H2
Howard St
St. Enoch 64 A2
Shop Cen
St. Enoch Sq 63 H2
St. Georges Pl 59 G5
St. Georges Rd
St. Georges St 59 G4
St. James Rd 60 B6
St. John's Ct 63 E4
St. John's Quad 63 E4
St. John's Rd 63 E5
St. Joseph's Ct 60 D5
St. Joseph's Pl 60 D5
St. Joseph's Vw 60 D5
St. Luke's Pl 64 A3
St. Luke's Ter 64 A3
St. Margarets Pl 64 A2
Bridgegate
St. Marnock St 65 E3
St. Marys La 63 H1
West Nile St
St. Michael's Ct 65 G3
St. Michael's La
St. Michael's La 65 G3
St. Monance St 60 D1
St. Mungo Av 60 A6
St. Mungo Pl 60 B6
St. Ninian Ter 64 A3
Ballater St
St. Peters La 63 G1
Blythswood St
St. Peter's Path 59 G4
Braid St
St. Peters St 59 G4
St. Rollox Brae 60 C4
St. Vincent Cres 58 D6
St. Vincent Cres La 58 D6
St. Vincent La 59 G6
Hope St
St. Vincent Pl 64 A1
St. Vincent St 59 G6
St. Vincent Ter 59 F6
Salamanca St 65 H3
Salisbury St 63 H4
Salkeld St 63 H4
Salmona St 59 H2
Saltmarket 64 A2
Saltmarket Pl 64 A2
Bridgegate
Saltoun Gdns 58 D3
Roxburgh St
Saltoun La 58 D3
Saltoun St 58 C3
Sanda St 59 E2
Sandfield St 59 E1
Sandiefield Rd 64 A4
Sandmill St 61 E5
Sandringham La 58 D3
Kersland St
Sandyfaulds Sq 64 A4
Sandyfaulds St 64 B4
Sandyford Pl 59 F6
Sauchiehall St
Sandyford Pl La 59 E6
Sandyford St 58 C6

Sandy La 58 A4
Crawford St
Sandy Rd 58 A5
Sannox Gdns 61 F6
Saracen Head La 64 C2
Gallowgate
Saracen St 60 A3
Sardinia La 58 D3
Sardinia Ter 58 D3
Cecil St
Sauchiehall La 59 G6
Sauchiehall St
Sauchiehall St 59 G6
Savoy St 64 D4
Sawmillfield St 59 H4
Schipka Pas 64 B2
Gallowgate
Scone St 60 A3
Scotland St 63 F3
Scotland St W 63 E3
Scotsburn Rd 61 G2
Scotstoun Mill Rd 58 C5
Partick Br St
Scott St 59 G6
Seagrove St 65 H2
Seamore St 59 F4
Seath St 64 A6
Seaward La 63 E2
Seaward Pl 63 E4
Seaward St 63 F3
Second Gdns 62 A4
Seton Ter 64 D1
Shaftesbury St 59 F6
Shakespeare St 59 E1
Shamrock St 59 G5
New City Rd
Shanks St 59 E1
Shannon St 59 F1
Shawfield Dr 64 C6
Shawfield Ind Est 64 D6
Shawfield Rd 64 D5
Shaw St 58 A6
Shearer St 63 F2
Paisley Rd
Shelley St 58 A1
Sheppard St 60 C2
Cowlairs Rd
Sherbrooke Av 62 C5
Sherbrooke Dr 62 C4
Sherbrooke Gdns 62 C5
Shettleston Rd 65 G2
Shields Rd 63 F3
Shipbank La 64 A2
Clyde St
Shore St 64 D6
Shortridge St 59 E1
Shuna Pl 59 E1
Shuttle La 64 B1
George St
Shuttle St 64 B1
Sidland Rd 61 G1
Siemens Pl 61 F4
Siemens St 61 F4
Silverdale St 65 G4
Silverfir Ct 64 B5
Silverfir Pl
Silverfir Pl 64 B5
Silverfir St 64 B5
Silvergrove St 64 C3
Simpson St 59 F3
Skene Rd 62 B3
Slatefield Ct 65 E2
Slatefield St
Slatefield St 65 E2
Sloy St 60 B2
Snowdon Pl 64 B4
Benthall St
Snowdon St 64 B4
Benthall St
Society St 65 F3
Solway St 64 D6
Somerset Pl 59 F5
Somerset Pl Ms 59 F5
Sorby St 65 H3
Sorn St 65 F5

South Annandale St 63 H6
Southbank St 65 H3
Southcroft St 62 B1
South Frederick St 64 A1
Southloch Gdns 60 D3
Southloch St 60 D3
Southmuir Pl 58 D1
Southpark Av 58 D4
Southpark La 59 E4
Southpark Ter 59 E4
Southpark Av
South Portland St 63 H3
Southside Cres 63 H4
South Woodside Rd 59 F3
Spiers Wf 59 H4
Spoutmouth 64 B2
Gallowgate
Springbank St 59 F2
Springburn Rd 60 C4
Springburn Shop Cen 60 D2
Springburn Way 60 C2
Springfield Ct 64 A1
Buchanan St
Springfield Quay 63 F2
Springfield Rd 65 F5
Springkell Av 62 C5
Springkell Dr 62 B6
Springkell Gdns 62 C6
Springkell Gate 62 D6
Spring La 64 A5
Lawmoor St
Springvale Ter 60 C2
Spruce St 60 B1
Staffa St 61 F6
Stafford St 60 B5
Stag St 62 B1
Stair St 59 F2
Stamford St 65 F3
Stanley St 63 E3
Stanley St La 63 E3
Steel St 64 B2
Stevenson St 64 C2
Stewart St 59 H5
Stewartville St 58 B4
Stirlingfauld Pl 63 H3
Stirling Rd 60 B6
Stobcross Rd 58 D6
Stobcross St 63 F1
Stobcross Wynd 58 C6
Stockwell Pl 64 A2
Stockwell St 64 A2
Stonyhurst St 59 H2
Stratford St 58 D1
Strathbran St 65 H4
Strathclyde St 65 E6
Striven Gdns 59 F3
Stroma St 61 F4
Stromness St 63 G4
Stronend St 59 H1
Stronsay St 61 F4
Suffolk St 64 C2
Kent St
Summerfield St 65 F6
Summer St 64 D3
Summertown Rd 62 B1
Sunnybank St 65 F5
Sunnylaw St 59 H2
Surrey St 63 H4
Sussex St 63 E3
Sutherland Av 62 B5
Sutherland La 58 C4
Swanston St 65 E6
Swan St 60 A5
Sword St 64 D2
Sydenham La 58 B3
Crown Rd S
Sydenham Rd 58 C3
Sydney St 64 C2

Syriam Pl 60 D2
Syriam St
Syriam St 60 D2

T
Tamworth St 65 E3
Rimsdale St
Tannock St 59 H2
Taransay St 58 A6
Taylor Pl 60 B6
Taylor St 64 B1
Telephone La 58 C3
Templetons Business Cen 64 C3
Templeton St 64 C3
Terregles Av 62 B6
Terregles Cres 62 B6
Terregles Dr 62 C6
Teviot St 58 C6
Teviot Ter 59 E2
Sanda St
Tharsis St 60 D5
Third Gdns 62 A4
Thistle Ter 64 A4
Thomson St 65 E2
Thornbank St 58 C5
Thornbridge Av 58 C1
Balcarres Av
Thorncliffe Gdns 63 E6
Thorncliffe La 63 E6
Thornhill Path 65 H4
Crail St
Thornwood Av 58 A4
Thornwood Gdns 58 A4
Thornwood Pl 58 A3
Thurso St 58 C5
Dunaskin St
Tibbermore Rd 58 A3
Tillie St 59 F3
Tiree St 61 G4
Tobago Pl 64 D3
Tobago St 64 C3
Todd St 65 G1
Tollcross Rd 65 H3
Tontine La 64 B2
Torness St 58 C4
Torrance St 60 D2
Torridon Av 62 B5
Torridon Path 62 A5
Dumbreck Av
Torrisdale St 63 F6
Torr St 60 B2
Torryburn Rd 61 G2
Toryglen St 64 B6
Tower St 63 E3
Townmill Rd 60 D6
Townsend St 60 A5
Tradeston St 63 G3
Trafalgar St 64 D5
Trongate 64 A2
Troon St 65 F5
Trossachs Ct 59 G3
Trossachs St
Trossachs St 59 G3
Tullis Ct 64 C4
Tullis St 64 C4
Tunnel St 63 E1
Tureen St 64 C2
Turnberry Av 58 B3
Turnberry Rd
Turnberry Rd 58 A3
Turnbull St 64 B2
Turner Rd 60 D4
Turnlaw St 64 B4
Turriff St 63 H4
Tweed Cres 61 H5
Tyndrum St 60 A5

U
Union Pl 63 H1
Gordon St
Union St 63 H1
Unity Pl 59 G4
University Av 58 D4
University Gdns 58 D4

University of Glasgow 58 D4
University Pl 58 D4
Urrdale Rd 62 B3

V
Valleyfield St 60 C3
 Ayr St
Vasart Pl 59 F1
Vennard Gdns 63 E6
Vermont St 63 E3
Vicarfield Pl 62 B1
 Vicarfield St
Vicarfield St 62 B1
Victoria Br 64 A2
Victoria Circ 58 C3
Victoria Cres 58 C3
 Dowanside Rd
Victoria Cres La 58 C3
Victoria Cres Pl 58 C3
 Bowmont Ter
Victoria Cres Rd 58 C3
Victoria Cross 63 G6
Viewfield La 59 E4
Viewpark Av 61 F6
Vine St 58 B4
Vinicombe La 58 D3
Vinicombe St 58 D3
Vintner St 60 A4
Virginia Bldgs 64 A1
 Virginia St
Virginia Ct 64 A1
 Virginia St
Virginia Pl 64 A1
Virginia St 64 A1
Vulcan St 60 C2
 Springburn Way

W
Waddell Ct 64 B3
Waddell St 64 B4
Walker Ct 58 B5
Walker St 58 B5

Walkinshaw St 65 E4
Wallace St 63 G2
Wallacewell Cres 61 F1
Wallacewell Pl 61 F1
Wallacewell Rd 61 F1
Walls St 64 B1
Walmer Cres 62 C2
Walnut Cres 60 B1
Walnut Pl 60 B1
Walnut Rd 60 B1
Walter St 65 F1
Wanlock St 58 A6
Wardhill Rd 61 F1
Wardrop St 58 A6
Warnock St 60 C6
Warriston Cres 61 H6
Warriston St 61 H6
Warroch St 63 F1
Washington St 63 G1
Waterloo La 63 H1
 Waterloo St
Waterloo St 63 G1
Water Row 58 A6
Waterside Pl 64 B4
Waterside St 64 B4
Watson St 64 B2
Watt St 63 F2
Waverley Ter 65 E2
 Whitevale St
Weaver St 64 B1
Webster St 65 E5
Wellcroft Pl 63 H4
Wellfield St 60 D2
Wellington La 63 G1
Wellington St 63 H1
Wellpark St 64 C1
Westbank Ct 59 E4
Westbank La 59 E4
Westbank Quad 59 E4
Westbourne Gdns La 58 C2
Westbourne Gdns N 58 C2

Westbourne Gdns S 58 C2
Westbourne Gdns W 58 C2
Westbourne Rd 58 B2
Westbourne Ter La 58 B2
 Westbourne Rd
West Campbell St 63 G1
West End Pk St 59 F5
Wester Common Dr 59 G1
Wester Common Rd 59 G2
Wester Common Ter 59 H2
Westercraigs 64 D1
Westercraigs Ct 64 D1
 Westercraigs
West George La 59 G6
 Pitt St
West George St 59 G6
West Graham St 59 G5
West Greenhill Pl 59 E6
Westminster Gdns 58 D3
 Kersland St
Westminster Ter 59 E6
 Royal Ter
Westmoreland St 63 G6
Westmuir St 65 H3
West Nile St 63 H1
West Princes St 59 F4
West Regent La 59 H6
 Hope St
West Regent St 59 G6
Westside Gdns 58 B4
West St 63 G3
West Whitby St 65 G4
Whitefield Rd 62 C3
Whitehall St 63 F1
Whitehill Gdns 65 E1
Whitehill St 65 E1
Whitehill St La 65 E1
White St 58 B4

Whitevale St 65 E2
Whittingehame Gdns 58 A1
Whitworth Gate 59 G1
Williamson St 65 G4
William St 59 F6
Willowbank Cres 59 F4
 Woodlands Rd
Willowbank St 59 F4
Wilson St 64 A1
Wilton Cres 59 F3
Wilton Cres La 59 F3
Wilton Dr 59 F3
Wilton Gdns 59 F3
Wilton St 59 E3
Windmillcroft Quay 63 G2
Windsor St 59 G4
Windsor Ter 59 G4
Winifred St 61 H2
Winning Row 65 H3
Winton Dr 58 C1
Winton La 58 C1
Wishart St 64 C1
Woddrop St 65 F6
Wolseley St 64 B5
Woodhall St 65 F6
Woodlands Dr 59 F4
Woodlands Gate 59 F5
Woodlands Rd 59 F4
Woodlands Ter 59 E5
Woodrow Circ 62 D4
Woodrow Pl 62 C4
Woodrow Rd 62 D4
Woodside Cres 59 F5
Woodside Pl 59 F5
Woodside Pl La 59 F5
Woodside Ter 59 F5
Woodside Ter La 59 F5
Wood St 61 F6
Woodville Pk 62 B2
Woodville St 62 B2
Wyndford Dr 58 D1

Wyndford Pl 58 D1
 Wyndford Rd
Wyndford Rd 58 C1
Wyndham Ct 58 D2
 Wyndham St
Wyndham St 58 D2
Wyper Pl 64 D2

Y
Yarrow Gdns 59 F3
Yarrow Gdns La 59 F3
Yate St 65 F3
Yew Dr 61 E3
Yorkhill Par 58 C5
Yorkhill Quay 58 C6
Yorkhill St 58 D6
York St 63 G2
Young Ter 61 E2

Z
Zena Cres 61 G2
Zena Pl 61 H2
Zena St 61 H2